THE WORLDLY
PHII

D1541119

including
- *A Note on the Author*
- *Individual Chapter Summaries and Commentaries*
- *Final Summary and Evaluation of Work*
- *Definitions of Significant Terms and Concepts*
- *Selected Examination Questions*
- *A Guide to Further Reading*

by
Joseph M. Leon, M.A.
Tallahassee Junior College

and

Charles H. Patterson, Ph.D.
University of Nebraska

Cliffs Notes
INCORPORATED
LINCOLN, NEBRASKA   68501

Editor

Gary Carey, M.A.
University of Colorado

Consulting Editor

James L. Roberts, Ph.D.
Department of English
University of Nebraska

ISBN 0-8220-1385-1
© Copyright 1965, 1974
by
C. K. Hillegass
All Rights Reserved
Printed in U.S.A.

1988 Printing

Cliffs Notes, Inc.   Lincoln, Nebraska

CONTENTS

A NOTE ON THE AUTHOR 5

FOREWORD 6

SUMMARIES AND COMMENTARIES 7

CHAPTER I   Introduction 7

CHAPTER II   The Economic Revolution 7

CHAPTER III   The Wonderful World of Adam Smith . 13

CHAPTER IV   The Gloomy Presentiments of Parson
              Malthus and David Ricardo 19

CHAPTER V   The Visions of the Utopian Socialists . 25

CHAPTER VI   The Inexorable System of Karl Marx . 32

CHAPTER VII   The Victorian World and the
              Underworld of Economics 41

CHAPTER VIII The Savage Society of
              Thorstein Veblen 47

CHAPTER IX   The Heresies of John
              Maynard Keynes 53

CHAPTER X   The Modern World 59

CHAPTER XI   Beyond the Economic Revolution . . 67

FINAL SUMMARY AND EVALUATION OF WORK . . . 73

DEFINITIONS OF SIGNIFICANT TERMS
     AND CONCEPTS 74

SELECTED EXAMINATION QUESTIONS 81

A GUIDE TO FURTHER READINGS 85

A NOTE ON THE AUTHOR

Robert L. Heilbroner (b. 1919) received his A.B. degree from Harvard in 1940, graduating "summa cum laude" and Phi Beta Kappa in economics. During World War II he served in the Intelligence Service, primarily in the Far Eastern theater of operations. Following the war, he did graduate work at the New School for Social Research in New York City, where he teaches. He has been a practicing economist, both in government and business, and has lectured before the National War College and many business, university, and labor groups.

He achieved immediate recognition, both as a writer and economist, with the publication of his first book, *The Worldly Philosophers*. First published in 1953, it has been revised in 1961, 1967, and in 1972. The last revision contains a complete rewriting of Chapters X and XI. It has been printed in several foreign editions and has been widely used in colleges and universities in the United States.

In 1956 Heilbroner's *The Quest for Wealth* was published which was concerned with the origin and nature of man's drive for acquisition and its role in the money-directed society of today.

The Future as History followed in 1960. This was an attempt to predict the future trend of the world — particularly that of the United States — on the basis of what is known of the past and the present as Heilbroner saw it. In this book, Heilbroner took a dim view of American optimism over the world struggle of ideologies. He was not entirely pessimistic, but urged Americans to awaken to action before it was too late if they were concerned about what kind of world their grandchildren would live in.

In 1962 *The Making of Economic Society* appeared and examined the development of economic societies from the past to the present — including the slave system, medieval feudalism, the industrial revolution, and the market system.

Heilbroner's latest book, *The Great Ascent*, published in 1963, surveys the process of economic development of some one hundred emergent nations which are populated by approximately two billion people, and the relationship of that development to the modern Western nations — particularly to the United States. In it the author favors foreign aid, but only in so far as it will aid the promotion of trade among the nations — which he sees as particularly effective.

THE WORLDLY PHILOSOPHERS

FOREWORD

The Worldly Philosophers is an extremely well written and interesting work which the student should enjoy reading. Consequently, this guide is designed to be a supplement to the book itself, not a substitute.

That an adequate guide is a most helpful aid to the student is proven from classroom teaching experience. All too often the new student of the social sciences finds himself unfamiliar with the basic concepts and the historical developments that form the foundation for the elaboration of the ideas presented in the text. The student does not have time to look up "Mercantilism," "The Scientific Revolution," "The Renaissance," the "Commercial Revolution," the "Great Depression," etc., and yet these terms must be understood before the text may be fully understood.

Furthermore, this text presents a deep insight into the world of economic ideas, and many students find the bold and ingenious jumps from idea to idea so sweeping that it is difficult to adequately absorb them.

Finally, the subject matter of this book is economics — and apparently vast numbers of students are quick to agree with Carlyle's characterization of economics as "the dismal science." If the view is "dismal," then the comprehension is unclear.

The purpose of this guide is therefore threefold: to present a chapter-by-chapter summary which highlights the basic message of each chapter; to present a commentary on each chapter which furnishes certain necessary background information and further explains the relevance of the points summarized; and finally, to provide an over-all presentation and evaluation of a most valuable book which is neither "dismal" or "unclear."

THE WORLDLY PHILOSOPHERS
SUMMARIES AND COMMENTARIES

CHAPTER I
INTRODUCTION

Summary
The subject of the book is the "Great Economists" — those men whose words and thoughts on the creation and distribution of wealth have had such a tremendous impact that they have swayed and shaped the world.

The title of the book comes from the one common interest of these thinkers — these philosophers: man's drive for worldly wealth. Hence, "the worldly philosophers."

Oddly enough, the worldly philosophers, or economists, did not appear on the scene of world events until long after the advent of historians, philosophers, scientists, statesmen, artists, and political theorists. In fact, the world of the economists did not begin until the latter part of the 18th century (with Adam Smith).

Commentary
While these economists are not yet named, they are described by such intriguing characterizations as: "a madman," "a skeptic," "a tramp," etc. Among the identifications — which become apparent later as their ideas are presented — are:

"a philosopher" — Adam Smith
"a parson" — Thomas R. Malthus
"a stockbroker" — David Ricardo
"a nobleman" — Saint-Simon
"a madman" — Charles Fourier
"a revolutionary" — Karl Marx
"an aesthete" — John Maynard Keynes
"a tramp" — Henry George
"a skeptic" — Thornstein Veblen

CHAPTER II
THE ECONOMIC REVOLUTION

Summary

From the beginning of man's existence the problem of his survival has existed. That survival has always been dependent on the work and cooperation of other men. And since the individual man is self-centered, society's existence is constantly threatened by the possibility that men will not adopt necessary jobs and faithfully execute them indefinitely. If there were not enough miners to work the mines, or if most miners should suddenly decide to follow some other line of work; if the farmers in a society should decide to become fishermen; or if not enough students studied for and became doctors, or engineers, the economy would break down. In short, if the dependence of man upon his fellow man were to fail at any of several vital points in the economy, the community would face a catastrophe. During the span of civilized man's existence, only three effective—and quite distinct—ways have been found as a safeguard against such a catastrophe.

Tradition
The passing down of tasks (jobs) from generation to generation through custom—a carpenter's son becoming a carpenter also; a farmer's son a farmer, etc. (Examples: especially true of the Middle Ages, and still true today in many of the underdeveloped areas of the world.)

Central Authoritarian Rule
The enforcement of economic survival by absolute rule or dictatorship. (Example: the building of the pyramids in ancient history, and the carrying out of the Soviet Union's Five Year Plans in modern history.)

Throughout most of civilized man's history—for hundreds and hundreds of years—the problem of survival was solved by one or other of these two methods. And since either method was quite simple and needed no economic explanation, there was no need for economists. There was no economic puzzle to explain until the Economic Revolution brought the third way, the market system.

The Market System
A system where buyers and sellers transact business freely with the goal of making profits, motivated by *self-gain*. This is *"capitalism."*

The market system is not the simple exchange of goods (which exists in primitive societies), nor the commercial fairs of the Middle Ages. Nor is it a farmers' produce market, or a stock exchange. The market system is much more than that—it is a system which supports and maintains an entire society. It did not come into existence immediately, nor was it a preconceived plan of one man or of any group of men. It evolved slowly, without plan, and was brought into being only through the advent of the most far-reaching revolution of the western world—the Economic Revolution. Many factors combined to make that revolution possible, such as the breaking up of the manorial system, the decline of the guilds, the acceptance of the concepts of Land, Labor, and Capital, the effects of the Renaissance, the scientific discoveries, the voyages of discovery and exploration by Europeans, the emergence of the modern nation-states, and the Protestant Reformation which made the concept of "profit" acceptable.

The market system not only evolved slowly, but it emerged only after much bitter opposition to change by those forces which sought to maintain the "status quo" and their favorable positions therein. Nevertheless, as the essential concepts of Land, Labor, and Capital became accepted, and the profit motive became respectable, the market system came into being, and with that fact it was finally necessary for the economist to appear in order to satisfactorily explain the complex system. The attempted explanations of the "Bullionists" (16th and 17th century philosophers who called for the accumulation of gold), and of the new disciples of the school of "Political Arithmetick" (who emphasized commerce rather than gold) were insufficient to explain the whole system. Into the void stepped Adam Smith, with his amazing and quite adequate masterpiece, the *Inquiry into the Nature and Causes of the Wealth of Nations*.

Commentary

Another name for the system of *"Tradition"* is the *"Subsistence economy."* The basic unit is the family, clan, or tribe and each unit produces all that it needs and consumes all that it produces. A good example in fiction is Robinson Crusoe, and examples today are found in the poor peasant of India, and many rural areas of Africa, Asia, and Latin America. The question of who shall work, and at what, is settled by custom.

Another name for the system of *"Central authoritarian rule"* is "Planned economy." The means of production and the authority to make economic decisions belong to the state. Examples are such ancient states as Egypt and Babylonia, and the modern communist nations such as the Soviet Union.

In the *"market system,"* known as a *"market economy,"* economic decisions are highly decentralized: each member of the labor force makes his own choice of which job to follow; each household decides what to buy with its income; and each business concern decides what to produce, what production methods to use, and where to sell its product. Examples today are the United States, western Europe, and the British dominions. This is known as "capitalism" or the "free enterprise system" or the "private enterprise system." The word, "capitalism" comes from the central feature of the system being the use of "capital."

However, none of the three methods or systems exists in pure form, and such systems as those practiced today in the United States, Great Britain, or in the Soviet Union are better described as "Mixed economies" —containing elements of both the "Market economy" and the "Planned economy."

In order to clearly understand what is meant by "The Economic Revolution," and to understand the balance of the book, a few definitions are in order:

Economics
The study of the ways in which man makes a living; the study of human wants and their satisfaction; the science of wealth.

Economic System
The rules, laws, customs, and principles which govern the operation of an economy. Each economic system has its own peculiar problems and therefore produces its own solutions.

Economic Activity
All action concerned with the creation of goods and services to be in some way consumed.

Consumption
The process by which goods and services are utilized in satisfying man's needs and wants.

Production
The process of creating the goods or services to be consumed.

Distribution
   a. *"Physical"*
The process of getting these goods and services into the hands of those who need them or want them for consumption.

   b. *"Personal"*
The division of *income* among persons, classified by size.

   c. *"Functional"*
The division of *income* according to different types — wages, rent, interest, profit.

Basic Agents of Production of the Market System

Land
Natural resources.

Labor
Human effort

Capital
The physical necessities for production — buildings, machinery, tools, equipment, supplies.

(These are called by economists the "Factors of Production," and include a fourth factor: "Management" — for planning, coordinating, and directing production — although some economists consider this as being a specialized high-level kind of labor.)

The market system involves a high degree of economic activity, revolving around the production of goods and services, but the basic agents of production — Land, Labor, Capital — did not exist as abstract ideas in the minds of men until the Economic Revolution. Of course, there was land used for agriculture, and labor in the form of human beings doing physical labor, and capital as providing the necessary funds for buying and maintaining the land. However, society as a whole did not consider these terms as impersonal ideas in the modern sense of "Let's start a business — we need Land for the location of the factory, we need an available Labor force, and we must have the Capital to get all this going."

During the Middle Ages land existed in the form of estates, manors, and principalities but it was not generally "For Sale," as it provided the prestige and status around which the social life of the times revolved.

There were serfs, apprentices, and journeymen who "worked," but there was no labor market. The serfs were bound to the land of their masters, the lords. The apprentices and journeymen served the "master" and they were rigidly controlled by the guild regulations.

Capital funds, in the sense of private wealth only, existed but not with any idea of investing and "taking risks." The goal was "safety first," such as financing the wars and the household expenses of kings — a good example being that of the Fugger banking family of Bavaria. Advertising was forbidden, and the basis of price was the "just price."

So, without Land, Labor, and Capital there was no Production in the modern economic sense, and therefore no market system, and society in the Middle Ages was run by custom and tradition. All this was changed by the Economic Revolution which represented a radical departure in the commercial practices and concepts of the times. The following factors were responsible for the Economic Revolution which ushered in the market system.

The Renaissance
(1350-1600) — particularly through the decay of the restrictive religious spirit in favor of a skeptical, inquiring attitude.

The Scientific Revolution
(1500-1700) — laying the foundations for the Industrial Revolution.

Emergence of Nation-States
(15th, 16th, and 17th centuries) — giving rise to royal patronage for favored industries, maritime trade, and to common laws, common measurement, and common currencies.

The Age of Exploration and Discovery
(15th, 16th, and 17th centuries) — providing natural wealth in gold and silver, and raw resources from the colonies.

The Protestant Reformation
(1500-1648) — by encouraging enterprise, the investment of capital, and making "interest" and "profit" respectable.

The greatest single change necessary for the adoption of the market system — capitalism — was a radical change in the attitude of society toward profit (toward the idea of *self-gain*). *Without the profit motive there would be no capitalism — no market system.*

Certainly, the concepts of "money" and of "profit" are old, with the first coin used as currency dating back to Lydia and 600 B.C., and with the Greek philosophers such as Xenophon, Plato, and Aristotle being well aware of wealth, money, and profit. However, rather than emphasize any economic considerations, the ancient philosophers "looked down" on such topics and stressed such basic questions as What is Truth?, What is Good?, What is Evil?, What is God?, What is Life? Later, the Church and its philosophers such as St. Augustine and St. Thomas Aquinas were completely absorbed with the question of "the immortality of the Soul." Salvation was taught to be the all-important concern of society and the acquisition of material goods or riches was bitterly criticized. And so it was that the New Testament phrase, "For the love of money is the root of all evil." (I Timothy, VI, 10) became a block against the development of the market system — a system which emphasized self-gain and profit.

However, gradually, due to the factors listed above, the market system did come into being. The Renaissance encouraged a new individualism in economic affairs which contributed to the breakdown of the guild system and to the rise of the individual man of enterprise. Protestantism became a particularly strong factor in the change of concepts because Calvinism especially encouraged enterprise, some Calvinists seeing prosperity as a sign of election to grace, and poverty as evidence of damnation. Thus, the Protestant Reformation did away with the old concept of the "just price" and the ban against receiving interest on money loaned. Consequently, the loaning of money and the investment of capital became respectable, and Western society widely adopted the profit motive. Then, and only then, was the Economic Revolution complete.

Now it was necessary for the new market system to be explained, and for a philosophy to be developed about it. This was achieved by Adam Smith — the "Father of Modern Economics."

CHAPTER III

THE WONDERFUL WORLD OF ADAM SMITH

Summary

Adam Smith (1723-1790) was a quiet, scholarly Scotsman who taught first at Oxford University and then at the University of Glasgow. He had gained fame as a moral philosopher and during his lifetime his book, *The Theory of Moral Sentiments,* was considered by the critics to be his best work. Consequently, he was already well known before his actual masterpiece, *An Inquiry into the Nature and Causes of the Wealth of Nations* was published. An opportunity to travel throughout Europe for three years had presented itself when he was offered the position of traveling tutor to the stepson of Charles Townshend. In his tour of the Continent, Smith was able to meet the leading thinkers of the "Age of Enlightenment," and was particularly impressed with François Quesnay, the principal spokesman for the French "Physiocrats." During his European tour, Smith worked on his *Wealth of Nations* and after returning to Scotland devoted ten years to the completion of the book. It was published in 1776.

The *Wealth of Nations* is almost an encyclopedia, and certainly far more than just a textbook on economics. One critic has called it "a history and criticism of all European civilization." It includes a discussion of the division of labor, the origin and use of money, the prices of commodities, the wages of labor, the profits of stocks, the value of silver, the rent of land, and an account of the economic development of Europe since the fall of the Roman Empire—among many other subjects. Its 900 pages are heavy going, for often Smith labors on and on without drawing a concrete and obvious conclusion. It is not actually an "original" book in the sense that its basic ideas are original, for Smith referred to more than 100 authors in developing his arguments and he borrowed heavily from the "Physiocrats" and Quesnay—from whom he got the doctrine of "laissez faire" ("to be left alone"). However, it is a masterpiece as it presents, in one long sweep, a comprehensive picture of economic life. It was Smith who called England "a nation of shopkeepers," and the title of his book comes from his desire to promote the wealth of the nation. By "wealth" he meant the goods produced for all the people of the nation to consume.

Briefly, this was his economic message:

First, if society is not to depend on either tradition or authoritarian rule to guarantee its survival, how can it depend on the unregulated market system—on capitalism? What is it about the market system which will ensure society's survival? Smith's answer lies in his two *laws of the market.*

His *general thesis* is that *every human being is motivated primarily by self-interest — and this benefits society.* In fact, a desire for wealth is only one example, for the desire for self-gain is the driving power behind all of man's activities. Therefore, self-interest (profit) is what motivates men to do the necessary tasks for which society is willing to pay. Or, as Smith wrote: "It is not from the benevolence of the butcher, the brewer, or the baker that we expect our dinner, but from their regard to their self-interest." Thus, *self-interest,* or profits, *is the first law of the market.*

But how can each man's selfish desire for gain be beneficial to society? Would not the greedy take advantage of the public and the result be the ruthless exploitation of society by a few? No, says Smith, because by means of an "invisible hand" the individual, in the process of providing for his own economic interest, unintentionally contributes to the economic well-being of his society. How? Through *competition — the second law of the market.* The individual who charges too much for his product will soon find that competitors have slipped in to take away his business by offering more reasonable prices, and if he pays his help too little, he finds his workers hiring out to others who will pay more to get their services.

So, each man freely chooses his type of work in his society under the market system — becoming a butcher or a baker, or a brewer, etc. Through such a multitude of choices, society is benefited by having all its necessary tasks filled. The individual is attracted to his particular task by self-interest, and he is prevented from allowing his self-interest to gouge society by competition. Thus, *the two laws of the market* — self-interest and competition — react upon each other and are self-balancing, guaranteeing the survival of society.

Furthermore, the laws of the market not only insure that prices are competitive, but they also determine the quantities of goods produced. If, for example, explains Smith, the public demands more gloves than shoes, there will be a brisk business on gloves and little demand for shoes. Consequently, the prices of gloves will rise as the demand exceeds the supply and pushes the prices up. Prices of shoes will go down because the supply exceeds the demand. *Self-interest* steps in again to balance things up for since there are higher profits in the glove business now, and the need for a greater supply, new producers will enter into the manufacture of gloves and workers will move from the shoe factories to the glove factories. The result will be that glove production will rise and shoe production will fall — and before long we will have a balance again. As the supply of gloves grows and meets the demand, glove prices will fall, and as the supply of shoes becomes less than the demand for them, shoe prices will rise and this will lead to increased production of shoes. Self-interest and competition, acting against each other, have balanced things out.

Finally, the laws of the market also regulate the incomes of the producers. When profits in one type of business become unusually large, new producers are attracted to that business — until competition has reduced the surplus of profit. In the same way, labor's wages are regulated — workers being attracted to higher-pay industries until the supply of workers there lowers the pay-scale to that of comparable jobs elsewhere. By the same token, the reverse is true — when profits or wages are too low, producers or workers will leave that field for more lucrative areas until supply and demand are better adjusted.

But the key to the operation of the laws of the market is that the market is *self-regulating if left alone ("laissez faire")* so that competition can operate freely *without any government controls — and without any monopolies*.

Does capitalism — the market system — actually operate in this way? It most certainly did during Adam Smith's time, for the world of business was largely a world of atomistic competition — a world without Big Government, Big Business, or Big Labor. Today, of course, the capitalistic world is greatly different. However, in spite of having been greatly modified by the full impact of the Industrial Revolution (which Adam Smith did not foresee), the twin laws of self-interest and competition still form the basis of operation of the market system.

In his vision of the future, Adam Smith was optimistic. To him, the society of the market system was *dynamic* and moved progressively. He saw this vividly demonstrated through the tremendous gain in productivity which resulted from *the minute division and specialization of labor*. He enthusiastically reported an example from his visit to a pin factory which employed only ten men. With each man specializing in only one operation, the total output of all ten men was over 48,000 pins a day — whereas if each man were to handle all the steps himself which were involved in the manufacture of the completed pin, he could not produce more than twenty pins at most in a day, or a total production of no more than 200 pins. And this division of labor, reported Smith, had its origin among primitive peoples — where one person was able to make bows and arrows better than anyone else and specialized in this work, trading his products for cattle with others who specialized in that task.

In his vision of society moving progressively forward economically, Smith saw two additional fundamental, and evolutionary, "laws" which propelled the market system in an ever-ascending spiral of productivity. These laws he called the "Law of Accumulation" and the "Law of Population."

The *Law of Accumulation* meant *the accumulation of profits — to be put back into production*. By accumulating savings (profits), the capitalist could, and should, purchase additional machinery — which would provide for the further division and specialization of labor, with further tremendous gains in productivity. However, more machinery would mean more workers to work them and eventually this increased demand for workers would lead to higher and higher wages until profits would vanish and further accumulations be impossible. What was Smith's answer to this obstacle?

The *Law of Population* was his perfect solution. To Smith, labor, like any other commodity, was subject to demand. As the effect of the Law of Accumulation would be increased wages for the working class, *the numbers of the working class would be thereby increased* because higher wages would mean a higher standard of living and a decrease of malnutrition, poor living conditions, cold, and disease which had tended to keep labor's population down (in England the infant mortality rate among the lower classes was unbelievably high). As the population of the working class — labor — increased it would become a counter-force to the level of wages, pushing wages down. As the result of wages going down, profits for the capitalist would rise again, and accumulation could continue after all.

So these two evolutionary Laws formed an endless chain for society through which progress was inevitable. Progress would be inevitable because although the Law of Population would always depress wages back toward a subsistence level, it would only be *toward* but not all the way down to the subsistence level. So conditions would steadily improve all the while that further accumulations for further investment continued. What would be the final result — far, far off in the future? A paradise of hard work, with a great deal of real wealth, and with very little leisure time — a "wonderful" world. Unfortunately, the Laws of Accumulation and Population did not operate in the way in which Smith predicted.

Commentary

To fully understand why the *Wealth of Nations* was a revolutionary book, one must know something of the economy and the living conditions in England at the time that Adam Smith published his monumental survey. What kind of an England was it in 1776? It was an England which was just going into the second stage of capitalism. There have been three major stages of capitalism.

The *first stage* — known as *"Commercial Capitalism"* — occurred between 1450 and 1650 and was brought about by the five factors which were responsible for the Economic Revolution (reviewed above), and was especially affected by the geographical discoveries, colonization, and the great increase in overseas trade. At this time the early capitalists, protected by government controls, subsidies, and monopolies, made their *profits from the transportation of goods.*

The *second stage* began about 1750 and was made possible by the adoption of new sources of energy — primarily the steam engine — which enabled the factory system to develop through the use of machines for manufacturing, and which resulted in the rapid growth of wealth. This stage is known as *"Industrial Capitalism,"* as capitalists made their *profits from manufacturing*. It reached its height in England during the 1850's.

The *third stage* of capitalism began during the last decades of the nineteenth century. Due to the control and direction of industry by financiers, this stage is known as *"Financial Capitalism,"* with the *profits* coming *from the investment of finance capital*.

So the *Wealth of Nations* appeared in England at the time that the Industrial Revolution was just getting under way — a fact which was not apparent to either Adam Smith or to the capitalistic class of the day. In England practically every section of economic life was under strict government control. Prices, wages, and hours of work were fixed, even production was regulated, and foreign trade was completely dominated by the government. The government was controlled by the landed aristocracy and only they had the right to vote and to hold public office. The House of Lords was dominated by the great families of nobility, and election of the members of the less static House of Commons was entrusted to approximately 3% of the nation's population.

The conditions of the poor were horrible. Men and women, stripped to the waist, and children of seven and ten worked in the mines, and for the masses life was a brutal struggle for a most meager existence. With wool having become a profitable commodity, new pastures were needed for sheep and these pastures had to be enclosed. Now the process of *enclosure* — begun in the sixteenth century — was in full swing, with thousands and thousands of tenant-farmers thrown off the land in order to make room for the more profitable sheep. As much as 10% of England's twelve to thirteen million population was composed of paupers, but any suggestion of a more equitable distribution of wealth was violently opposed by the aristocratic ruling class. Temporary relief was one thing, but a "cure" was unthinkable for the poor were considered to be a necessary segment of a stable society.

The dominant economic concept of the day — maintained by the government and supported by the business interests of the day — was *"Mercantilism."* Upholding the view of the "Bullionists" that the real wealth of the nation consisted of gold and silver (bullion), the Mercantilists had since Henry VIII made State control a vital part of their doctrine. Their basic goal was to achieve a strong, self-sufficient economy, protected by a strong central government. The program called for (1) accumulation of gold and silver, (2) a "favorable" balance of trade through an excess of exports to imports, (3) the self-sufficiency of the nation by the provision of raw materials from within the country, or failing that, through colonies, (4) colonies to be not only the source of such raw materials but to serve as an export market for the nation's manufactured goods, (5) low wages for labor with long hours of work, (6) high tariffs to protect home industries and to discourage imports and (7) a strong merchant marine.

The *Wealth of Nations* launched a specific attack on the doctrine of Mercantilism. In the celebrated section, "Book IV," Adam Smith called for free trade, both domestic and foreign, advocating the abolishing of duties, bounties, prohibitions, and trading monopolies. Forget "balance of trade," he argued. "Wealth does not consist in money, or in gold and silver, but in what money purchases, and is valuable only for purchasing." Thus, the real wealth of nations consists of the goods which they can produce and trade, and this can only be accomplished by allowing production and commerce to develop freely, without any controls. In short, this was a brilliant exposition of economic "laissez faire" — for business to be left alone. Smith was indebted to the "Physiocrats" for the concept of "laissez faire," but while they had maintained that the real wealth of a nation came from its land and agriculture, he saw wealth as consisting of the manufacture of goods dependent on labor. As opposed to the emphasis on agriculture by the "Physiocrats," Smith emphasized manufacture.

The substitution of the doctrine of "laissez faire" for that of "Mercantilism" did not come immediately with the publication of the *Wealth of Nations* however. It was during the following century — the nineteenth — that the *Wealth of Nations* made its full impact, and then Great Britain discarded "Mercantilism" completely to become the world's wealthiest nation. When recognition came it came from the rising industrial capitalists who made the *Wealth of Nations* their economic "Bible," disregarding of course, any unkind words which Smith had written about them, such as: "People of the same trade seldom meet together but the conversation ends in a conspiracy against the public, or in some diversion to raise prices..."

Adam Smith, in fact, was neither pro-capital nor pro-labor. While at the University of Glasgow he had early come under the influence of Francis Hutcheson who first voiced the phrase, "the greatest happiness of the greatest number" (expounded on later by Jeremy Bentham), and this concept was dominant in the mind of Smith as he surveyed mankind. He was not an apologist for the capitalists, for while admiring their working ability, he was suspicious of their motives, and he called for high wages for labor. In writing of the poor, he wrote: "No society can surely be flourishing and happy, of which by far the greater part of the numbers are poor and miserable." Consequently, it was not his desire to take sides with any class — in his book he is only concerned with promoting the wealth of all classes, of the entire nation.

One principle which Smith stated, and which none of the capitalists who used the *Wealth of Nations* as an argument in favor of their special interests ever mentioned, was his concept of labor value. His observation that labor is the only real standard of the value of all products has been contradicted by most economists, but widely adopted by socialist writers. Some ninety years later Karl Marx was to seize and expand upon this idea, building it into his exaggerated theory of "surplus value."

What the British capitalists stressed was Smith's gospel of "laissez faire." Ignoring the fact that the great enemy to Smith's vision of the market system was *monopoly* in any form — government or otherwise — they found justification for their resistance to the first government attempts at social legislation. At the time children were shackled to machines in the factories where they worked and child labor was a common feature of the poorly ventilated and unsanitary factories. When laws were proposed to abolish the worst of these practices the factory owners quoted the *Wealth of Nations* in defense of being left unregulated. And so it was that Adam Smith's proposals for measures to protect the worker, the farmer, the consumer, and society at large; his suggestion that Slavery be abolished; his warning that Government should step in whenever necessary to prevent the formation of business monopolies which would lead to the restraint of free, competitive trade; his call for government support of general education for the people — were all ignored by the capitalists who championed the *Wealth of Nations* as the vindication of their business practices. And so it was that this quiet, peaceful scholar became for the capitalistic world the "Patron Saint of Free Enterprise."

Beyond that, Adam Smith, by thoroughly describing and explaining the market system, became the *"Father of Modern Economics."* In doing so, he founded the school of the "Classical Economists" — whose chief spokesmen were David Ricardo and Thomas Malthus.

CHAPTER IV

THE GLOOMY WORLD OF
PARSON MALTHUS AND DAVID RICARDO

Summary
Adam Smith's vision of the world had been one of glowing optimism when he founded the school of "Classical Economists." Ironically, the chief spokesmen for that school — David Ricardo and Thomas Malthus — while accepting the principles which Smith had laid down, differed sharply from him in their pessimistic view of that world. Each — in his own way — saw a gloomy world whose future was dismal and bleak. Ricardo and Malthus were contemporary British economists who violently disagreed with each other's economic views on practically every point — except one. When one would publish a book or an article developing a particular economic thesis, the other would soon publicly attack it. Yet they held a very high personal regard for one another and were good friends, never attacking each other

personally. Not only did they differ in their economic views, but their personal fortune and way of life differed greatly.

David Ricardo was a successful stockbroker who at the age of 26 had become financially independent. He won widespread respect and his social position was very high, including membership in Parliament where he earned the epithet, "the man who educated Commons." His *Principles of Political Economy* helped make him the outstanding economist of his day. While most practical in financial matters, he was essentially a theorist when writing on economics.

The Reverend Thomas Malthus had none of Ricardo's good fortune and social success. On the contrary, he never enjoyed anything more than a quite modest income and he was continually criticized for his ideas. In fact, his biographer called him "the best abused man of his age." Spending most of his life engaged in academic research, Malthus became *the first professional economist*. Not at all practical in financial matters, he was most practical in his economic views.

DAVID RICARDO (1772-1823)

In the forty years that had passed since the publication of the *Wealth of Nations,* the English economic scene had become dominated by the clash between the interests of the rising industrial capitalists and those of the conservative and complacent landed aristocracy. These interests particularly clashed over the matter of food prices. Since the capitalist had to pay at least a subsistence wage to his workers, he was vitally interested in keeping the price of food low. To this end he encouraged the importation of cheap wheat and corn from abroad. The landowner—the landlord—naturally resented this as it depressed the prices and profits of his own wheat and corn. The landlord's resentment was translated into action in Parliament where he, and not the capitalist, was represented. The result was the passage of the "Corn Laws" which imposed a sliding scale of duties on imported grains—thereby effectively keeping low-priced grains out of England. And the political power of the landlord (the landed aristocracy) was so great that these Corn Laws were not repealed until thirty years later.

Observing the advantageous position of the landlord, and the struggle of the competing capitalists, and also noting the economic plight of the worker, David Ricardo saw a dismal and pessimistic future for capitalism. While to Adam Smith society had been one happy family with the "Invisible Hand" providing for all, to Ricardo society was a bitter competitive contest which could only end in tragedy. He viewed the worker as little more than a robot, whose only human expression was his indulgence in family sex life. Instead of improving his standard of living when his wages tended to rise, the worker spent more time in bed and thereby increased the labor supply—

which would offset the tendency for wages to rise as this supply met and exceeded the demand for workers. Thus, the worker was doomed to gain no more than *a subsistence level of wages.*

As for the capitalist, Ricardo saw him as eternally seeking profits but engaged all the while in fierce competiton with other capitalists—which would naturally keep profits down. Worse, the capitalist was further squeezed by the landlord, for since profits depended largely on the amount of wages which had to be paid, the high price of grains would always result in high food prices which would mean high wages. While Ricardo considered the roles of the worker and the capitalist in the market system to be legitimate, he saw *the landlord as the villain.*

Ricardo's *Theory of Rent* entered into this dismal description of society. He explained rent—the landlord's income—as a very special kind of return which originated from the differences in cost between productive land and less productive land. In other words, the *yield* would be so much *greater* from productive land that *its cost of production* would be much, much *less* than that of less productive land. *This difference in costs* would be represented in *rent,* for selling price of the product—artifically high due to great demand and to no competition from imported grains—would be the same for both yields. This rent—the landlord's income from the return for the grains cultivated on his land—was not controlled or restricted by the free competition of the market, said Ricardo, because the land did not change hands. Thus, he viewed the landlords as possessing monopolies. As the economy progressed and the population increased, new lands of cultivation would be needed to meet the increased demand for the grains necessary to feed that population. This would push the selling price of grain up and increase the income of the landlord. And this increased income would be at the expense of the capitalist—who had to pay increased wages for the workers to be able to buy enough food for them to exist. Therefore, concluded Ricardo, of the three parties in this bitter struggle—the worker, the capitalist, and the landlord—only the landlord would profit as the economy expanded.

As to the future, it was to be a most dismal one as the worker was doomed to a subsistence wage through his lack of sexual restraint, and the capitalist would have his profits gobbled up by the landlord. Ironically, due to his financial investments Ricardo was himself a landlord. However, this did not prevent him from attacking what he saw as an evil, and he continually sought the abolition of the Corn Laws. As a result *David Ricardo became the champion of the rising capitalists.*

Commentary
A little over twenty years after the death of David Ricardo the Corn Laws were abolished (1846) and the industrial capitalists eventually broke the power of the landlords and replaced them in dominating British

society. Consequently, the dismal future which Ricardo had envisioned did not come to pass.

Ricardo's main contributions were two. His *Theory of Rent* was based on the new concept that rent arises from differences in the quality of land, and therefore arises from the *scantiness* of Nature. This was a direct refutation of the concept of the "Physiocrats" that rent arose from the *bountifulness* of Nature.

Of greater importance was Ricardo's theory of labor's wages. While not called as such in the text, this is what the German socialist, Ferdinand Lassalle, labeled the "Iron Law of Wages" — which stated that labor's wages must remain at the subsistence level (as explained above). *This subsistence level,* said Ricardo, *is labor's "natural price"* — that income which is necessary for the worker to barely exist (subsist) and at the same time perpetuate his stock. By applying the doctrine of "laissez faire" to this concept, Ricardo argued that wages should be left to the free competition of the market and should never be controlled by the interference of government. And this argument was taken up by the capitalists.

THOMAS R. MALTHUS (1766-1834)

Summary

Oddly enough, since his income was quite modest and he was certainly no landlord, Thomas Malthus defended the landlord and attacked Ricardo's views. Instead of viewing the landlord as a villain, Malthus praised him as being an ingenious capitalist in his own right. However, Malthus was also pessimistic over the future of capitalism, but for a different reason. He warned of *"general gluts,"* explaining that the process of saving might lead to lessened demand for goods (less money in circulation) and thereby to an excessive quantity of products without enough buyers. Although this fear was logically refuted by Ricardo, it does show that Malthus was far ahead of his time in predicting *depressions*.

While motivated by a sincere interest in the welfare of the poor, Malthus earned a torrent of criticism by opposing relief and housing projects for the poor — objecting to these measures on the grounds that such charity was only cruelty in disguise. His reasoning was that by keeping the poor man alive the result would be that he would then propagate his own kind — have children who would also be poor — and this was cruel.

It was not, however, his many articles on economics, nor his *Principles of Political Economy* (same title as Ricardo's book) which made the Reverend Thomas R. Malthus famous. It was his anonymously published (1798) *An Essay on the Principles of Population as It Affects the Future Improvement of Society,* whose reception was so great that Malthus expanded the original first edition of only 50,000 words into a second edition of well over 600 pages. The effect was to change Adam Smith's optimistic world to a world so dismal that upon reading Malthus, Thomas Carlyle exclaimed that economics was "the dismal science." Scorn and derision were heaped upon "Parson" Malthus as a result. Yet, approval came from an unexpected quarter, for on what Malthus had to say about population, David Ricardo was in full agreement.

The inspiration for Malthus' masterpiece came from his reading of the incorrigibly optimistic *Political Justice* of William Godwin. Godwin's vision of the future was a Utopia in which there would be no war, no crime, no disease, no government, and nothing but complete happiness. Malthus' dissenting views became the *Essay on Population*.

Malthus' thesis—known as the *"Malthusian Doctrine"*—is simply that population, unless checked, grows at a greater rate than the means of subsistence (the ability to feed that population). If unchecked, this population rate of growth would result in the population of the world being doubled every twenty-five years. Being the first economic statistician, Malthus based this twenty-five year period on the statistics of the population growth of the United States (where a real census appeared before it did in England) which showed that the United States population had doubled in twenty-five years. So, explained Malthus, population would continue to increase *geometrically,* doubling itself, as the numbers 1, 2, 4, 8, 16, 32, etc. Why could not the means of subsistence keep pace? Simply because land—the basis of agriculture—was added to cultivation in units of one additional section at a time. In other words, the means of subsistence could only increase *arithmetically,* as the numbers 1, 2, 3, 4, 5, 6, etc. Clearly, the result would be too many people, with not enough food to feed them. That is, if population growth continued *unchecked.*

How could population be checked? First, by *positive checks*—which had been present throughout history. They were war, disease, infanticide (killing off of infants), poverty, and famine. With the present rate of population growth, it was obvious that the positive checks had not halted this population trend. Second, there were the *preventive checks* of sexual abstinence and vice. What Malthus advocated as the only possible solution was abstinence, or what he called "moral restraint." He called for late marriages as fertility would be lessened in the later years and the passions of youth would have "cooled off" to a great extent. Being a minister, he could hardly advocate vice, so he more and more stressed the advantages of "moral restraint." However, the Reverend was a most practical observer of human conduct and he showed no confidence in the ability of men and women to actually practice this "moral restraint" to a sufficient degree. Consequently, his vision of the future was a most dismal one for he believed that the future of mankind would be *starvation* from famine. While aware of direct birth control practices, he disapproved of them on moral grounds.

Were Malthus' basic facts correct? Yes, they were—as is shown by the actual rate of population growth in much of the world today, as in India and China. Why, then, did his dismal prediction not come to pass? Basically, due to two main factors. First, the widespread use of modern birth control measures—particularly in the Western world—and secondly, to the tremendous increases in agricultural technology which provided more than enough food in the advanced countries. Birth control, ironically, was originally called "Neo-Malthusianism."

Commentary

While the majority of economists and scientists today consider the Malthusian Doctrine to be invalid, an increasing number of demographers (scientists who study population statistics) warn that it is very real indeed. Less than 20% of the world's peoples depend largely on preventive checks, and these live in the more advanced areas of the world, such as Europe and the United States. It is just where population explosions have been taking place—in the "backward" areas—that only positive checks have been applied. Further, in such areas as India and China, and portions of Latin America, the increased use of modern sanitation, hygiene, and preventive medicine has increased the problem of over-population by reducing the high death rates caused by the positive checks.

Malthus made his startling observation in 1798, before the appearance of numerous population explosions. The sober facts are these. While for twelve centuries (from 600 to 1800) the total population of Europe was never greater than 180 million, from 1800 to 1914 Europe's population jumped from 180 million to 460 million! That Malthus was not as incorrect in his analysis as modern economists would have us believe is shown by the fact that since his death the world's population has been doubling every thirty-five years—but as of 1964 it is doubling every *twenty-five years*. In the modern nation of Costa Rica, where birthrates are high and death-rates are low, the population growth is booming, uncontrolled. In China, where 75% of all deaths are due to preventable diseases, the present birth-rate is such—even without the application of modern medicine and sanitation—that in less than 100 years its population will be over five billion. So, the Malthusian Doctrine is a specter that haunts the minds of an increasingly respectable minority of scholars—even if not of the majority of writers, including the author of the text.

In any event, the warnings of the chief spokesmen for the school of "Classical Economists" swayed the minds of their generation, and the "wonderful world" of Adam Smith became the "gloomy world" of Thomas Malthus and David Ricardo—paving the way for the appearance of the "Utopian Socialists."

CHAPTER V

THE BEAUTIFUL WORLD
OF THE UTOPIAN SOCIALISTS

Summary
"Gloomy" was an adjective not only for the future world described by Malthus and Ricardo, but a fit description for the actual world of England in the 1820's. England had been victorious in the long struggle of the Napoleonic Wars on the Continent, but at home she was wallowing in the social evils of the factory system. Working conditions in the factories were terrible—unbelievable by our present-day standards. Boys and girls of ten years, and less, worked in such industrial centers as Manchester and Birmingham in buildings poorly ventilated and lacking the most basic sanitary and safety measures. The new machines were not fenced off and horrible cases of mangling of the workers by machines were a common occurrence. With no system of workmen's compensation or health insurance, an injured worker was likely to be thrown out into the street, destitute. It was not unusual for children to be whipped, not only for the slightest mistake, but also to "stimulate" them to greater efficiency. In some places the children scrambled with the pigs for slops of food. A sixteen-hour working day was common—from six in the morning to ten at night—and many children spent their few hours of sleep in cots in the unsanitary factory itself. Such conditions were described by magazine articles in *The Lion,* in the novels of Charles Kingsley and Charles Dickens, and by such critics of the factory system as John Ruskin and Thomas Carlyle, and even documented by government investigating commissions.

In the midst of this picture of despair, there suddenly appeared in unbelievable contrast an almost unbelievable man, Robert Owen.

ROBERT OWEN (1771-1858)

The early life of Robert Owen was a Horatio Alger story of personal success. Born into a poor Welsh family, Owen's schooling was interrupted when he became an apprentice worker at the age of nine. When he was eighteen and then living in England, he borrowed a small amount of money and set himself up as a capitalist, manufacturing machinery for the textile industry—a very small capitalist, to be sure, but a capitalist nevertheless. Not long after, he boldly applied for—and received—the position of factory manager of a large spinning mill, even though he had no knowledge of the work. By the time he was twenty he had succeeded in becoming the "boy wonder" of the textile industry. A few years later, with borrowed capital, he bought a group of textile mills at New Lanark, Scotland—and with these he made a fortune.

What was revolutionary, however, was the manner in which Robert Owen operated these mills. He completely eliminated the typical social evils of the British factory system and transformed New Lanark into *a model workers' community.* He did this by raising wages, reducing the hours of work, improving factory sanitation, rebuilding the workingmen's homes, and even by providing schools for the workers' children. And in the process he upset the standard concept of labor relations which the industrial capitalists held—for in improving working conditions Owen gained greater productivity and factory efficiency, which returned higher profits. So he proved that a concern by the capitalist for the conditions of the working class was not unprofitable—a fact, however, which the typical capitalist of the time found exceedingly difficult to accept. In essence, New Lanark became for Owen a laboratory in which he could test his philosophy.

What was his philosophy? It was that mankind was no better than its environment. Since man *was therefore shaped by his environment,* the proper thing to do was to improve that environment. With the right surroundings, then, a paradise on earth could be achieved. In developing this concept in talks with business and government leaders, Owen shocked them by stating that the development of machine production, if organized entirely for profit, would inevitably lead to the poverty and degradation of the working class. His solution was cooperation, and he invisioned *"Villages of Cooperation"*—planned communities where from eight hundred to twelve hundred persons worked together. The families would live in private apartments within houses grouped together in "parallelograms" (a quadrilateral with opposite sides equal). Kitchens and sitting rooms and all the means of production necessary for the welfare of the group would be owned and used in common. The community would be chiefly agricultural, but would carry on a variety of occupations which would insure self-sufficiency, and in the distance would be a factory unit.

Naturally, since the concept of "laissez faire" was now in full vogue, very few persons took Owen's proposal seriously, and in spite of Ricardo being willing to try the plan, the necessary funds and support were not forthcoming. Undaunted, Owen decided to go it alone and he sold his New Lanark holdings in order to finance such a project in the United States. On the fourth of July, 1826, in Indiana, "New Harmony" was set up as a "Village of Cooperation." As often happens with idealists, Owen did not choose his associates well and allowed the project to spring up with very little practical planning. One associate defrauded him, rival communities began to spring up, and the final result was the complete failure of the New Harmony experiment, with the loss by Owen of 80% of his entire fortune. Owen sold the land and after being unable to interest either President Jackson of the United States or Santa Ana of Mexico in another venture, he returned to England.

Yet, Owen did not change his views—which included a profound distrust of money and of private property. His philosophy had made a deep impression on the working class, and based on his teachings there began to spring up throughout England a series of producers' cooperatives and consumers' cooperatives, with some attempts at money-less exchanges. What finally survived—right down to this day—was *the consumer cooperative movement*—begun by a group of twenty-eight men who called themselves the *"Rochdale Pioneers."* This was the indirect result of Owen's philosophy but Owen was not involved directly because he had launched into a moral crusade for the working class. At the head of the English leaders of the working-class movement he formed a huge "Grand National" union which officially began its program in 1833 with a membership of half a million workers. This was the forerunner of the modern industrial trades-union but Owen's program called for a wide social change. He sought better wages and better working conditions, the setting up of "Villages of Cooperation," and the abolition of money. Owen travelled over the countryside, advocating the trades-union program in what was his final cause. Within two years it was a complete failure for the obstacles were too many. Not only did the government disrupt the movement through anti-union legislation, but local unions could not control their members—and to make matters worse, Owen and his lieutenants quarreled and broke off their association.

So at the age of 64, Robert Owen, the successful capitalist who did not believe in capitalism, found his utopian projects ended in failure. However, he did not wither away and die, but continued publicizing his ideas and even found the time to write his *Autobiography*. Finally, at the age of 87, still optimistic, he died. He had been the most romantic of the "Utopians" and he had swayed the minds of men by proving by direct action that industrial capitalism could sponsor humanitarian working conditions and still make profits.

Commentary

Robert Owen is known as the "Founder of British socialism." In fact, it was he who first used the words, "socialist" and "communist." His concept of socialism was not, however, the class warfare concept of Karl Marx but rather, a concept in the utopian fashion of the early utopian writers (see below at end of this chapter). His philosophy of socialism passed down to the "Fabian Society" of Great Britain—whose leaders were George Bernard Shaw, Sidney and Beatrice Webb, and H. G. Wells—and finally down to the Labour Party of Great Britain, which is a moderate socialist party. So the legacy of Owen includes British socialism, the passage of factory legislation in his time to correct the deplorable working conditions, the modern trades-union, and the modern consumer cooperative.

SAINT-SIMON (1760-1825)

Summary

The Count Henri de Saint-Simon was a French aristocrat who was imbued with the spirit of democracy and who had translated his convictions into action by participating in the American Revolution. He was known for his "pigheadedness" and this characteristic was manifested in a fantastic survey of knowledge which dissipated his finances. This search for knowledge was culminated by Saint-Simon's belief in the "Brotherhood of Man," and what he actually founded was an industrial religion.

What this half-mad "Utopian" stressed was the necessity for man to work, and as a consequence he maintained that it was the workers who deserved the greatest rewards from society, and the idlers who should receive the least. But in looking about him, Saint-Simon found the opposite to be true—it was the non-working aristocracy who received the greatest share of the wealth, and while doing the least work. His solution was the reorganization of society along the lines of a factory, with the function of government being economic rather than political. The government should arrange things with the help of scientists, technicians, and capitalists in such a way that rewards would be given in proportion to one's social contribution. Rewards should go to the active members of the factory and not to the lazy onlookers. But Saint-Simon offered only a theoretical solution, without working out any of the practical steps. After his death his ideas degenerated into a mystical, hazy sort of religion, with churches in France and branches in England and Germany.

Commentary
Saint-Simon, while quite impractical, is generally credited as being the "Founder of French socialism." Defining a nation as "nothing but a great industrial society," and politics as "the science of production," he took as his motto: "Everything by industry; everything for industry."

CHARLES FOURIER (1772-1837)

Summary
If Saint-Simon was half-mad, then his countryman, Charles Fourier, was altogether mad. He believed that the total life of the earth was to be 80,000 years—consisting of 40,000 years of "ascending vibrations" and 40,000 years of "descending vibrations." There were altogether eight stages of advancement for Man. We had already passed through the stages of "Confusion," "Savagery," "Patriarchism," and "Barbarousness," and were now living in the stage of "Happiness" ("Bonheur"). As we attained the stage of "Harmony" the sea would become lemonade and we would each live to be 144 years old—of which 120 years would be spent in the unrestricted delights of sexual love. The ascending and descending vibrations would find the eight stages repeated over and over again. In spite of his optimistic vision of the future, Fourier saw the practical world as being utterly disorganized and he proposed in minute detail a utopian solution.

The solution was to reorganize society into *"phalanxes"* — an organized community of some 1800 persons living together under one roof, as in a super hotel. There would be as much privacy as each person desired, and the style of living would vary with one's ability to pay. There would be agricultural workers, mechanics, and craftsmen — and everyone would have to work. However, one would work only a few hours each day and only at what he liked best. As for dirty work, why, the children would be glad to do that. Throughout, there would be a spirit of competition to see who did the best work. Fourier believed that the "phalanx" would be quite profitable with profits running as high as 30% of the investment. All such profits would be shared, but divided on the basis of 5/12 to labor, 4/12 to capital, and 3/12 to "ability" ("talent"), and everyone would be urged to become a part owner as well as a fellow worker.

Surprisingly, the idea spread and in the United States alone there were over forty phalanxes ("phalansteries"), including the Brook Farm colony in Massachusetts. However, while some lasted for several years, none was permanent.

Commentary
The one thing which the Utopian Socialists had in common was that they were dreamers who dreamed of the betterment of mankind. Some of their dreams, such as those of Fourier in particular, were quite ridiculous. Yet, as Shakespeare said, "We are such stuff as dreams are made on..."; and it takes dreams to stimulate men to attain progress. Of these Utopians, Robert Owen's contributions were the most practical and the most lasting, but all of these men dared to be different and to present their dreams to a scoffing world. It is important to note that these thinkers were both "Utopians" and "Socialists" — meaning that they were economic reformers who attempted to bring an ideal society into existence by changing their present society. To understand their role, an explanation of several terms is in order.

Utopia
A term used to describe any social, intellectual, or political scheme which is impractical at the time when it is conceived and presented. It is also used to refer to those *ideal states* which are impossible to realize because they are peopled by ideal human beings, and because they are based generally on what the author thinks *ought to be,* rather than on what actually is. There have been such famous examples as Plato's *Republic,* Sir Thomas More's *Utopia* (from where the name comes), Sir Francis Bacon's *New Atlantis,* and Campanella's *City of the Sun.*

Socialism
Means the state ownership of the basic means of production. The fundamental objective of socialism is the prevention of the exploitation of the vast numbers of workers who are dependent on the capitalists and the

landlords. Socialists believe that the wealth produced should be distributed more equally, and that distribution under capitalism is unfair. Their solution is the nationalization of all land, forests, and minerals, all means of production, transportation, trade, and banking—with the profits which formerly went to the capitalists and landlords to go to the people as a whole, through the State. Rent and interest would be abolished, as would the leisure class, and all citizens would work according to the best of their ability. Private property in the form of clothing, household possessions, money, and perhaps a house and a small plot of land would be allowed the individual, but all else would be owned collectively. This is, of course, the modern concept of socialism which has evolved over the years, based on the concept of common ownership—which is an old concept, going back to Plato's *Republic,* More's *Utopia,* etc. As already noted, the term was first used in England by Robert Owen. But, as contrasted with "communism"—and this is a very big "but"—the socialists believe in attaining their goals by *an evolutionary process,* through the democratic means of the ballot. Consequently, socialists believe in, and practice democracy.

Communism

This will be covered in the next chapter, but basically it differs from socialism in its method of attaining the same goal. Its method is a *revolutionary* one, and in the process it sets up *class warfare.*

Utopian Socialists

Reformers who were inspired largely by the ideas of the "Enlightenment" and the French Revolution, particularly the belief in progress and in the perfectibility of man. They did not preach class hatred but instead appealed to the intellectual and capitalistic classes to reform society voluntarily. Ironically, their name came from Karl Marx who used it as a term of scorn, saying that these reformers were nothing more than impractical idealists, calling for a Utopia—thus they were "Utopian Socialists" rather than his brand of practical "revolutionary socialists." From them came the concept of the "welfare state," held by the modern-day socialists of Great Britain and the Scandinavian countries, as well as others.

The last economist to be taken up in this chapter—John Stuart Mill—was not actually a "Utopian Socialist" but rather the champion of "Democratic Liberalism," which was a broad-minded view of the principles of "laissez faire," and often called "economic liberalism." However, Mill gradually came closer and closer to the socialist point of view and in doing so he added respectability to the ideas of the Utopian Socialists.

JOHN STUART MILL (1806-1873)

Summary

John Stuart Mill was the son of James Mill—a famous economist, philosopher, and historian, a friend of David Ricardo, and a champion of "laissez faire." The father personally handled the education of his son and John Stuart Mill began to learn Greek at the *age of three!* When he was eight he began the study of Latin, and by the time he was twelve he had read all the outstanding Greek and Roman classics (in the original), and the great English works of philosophy and history. He had also absorbed geometry, algebra, and differential calculus, and had written several books on history. By the age of thirteen he had mastered logic and had read all the major works on economics.

He did not write his major work on economics until some thirty years later, and in the meantime fell in love with Mrs. Harriet Taylor. Since she was a married woman and this was an age of respectability, their romance for the next twenty years was a platonic one even though they travelled together for a good part of that time. Upon the death of the husband they were happily married. With the publication in 1848 of his two-volume economic masterpiece, *Principles of Political Economy*, John Stuart Mill was recognized as the greatest economist of his age. The significance of this work was that in it he broke away from the economic philosophy of his father and dealt a severe blow to the concept of "laissez faire." In surveying the entire field of economics, Mill made an economic "discovery"—the thesis that the economic "laws" of the Classical Economists only applied to production and had nothing to do with *the distribution of wealth.* He argued that the distribution of wealth depended on the customs and laws of each society and that therefore there was no one "right" way of distributing that wealth. Each society could adopt whatever method of distribution it might wish. This was indeed a profound discovery—for it meant that *society could distribute its wealth on the basis of ethics and morality,* instead of being bound by cold and impersonal "inevitable laws."

In contrast to the "gloomy world" of Malthus and Ricardo, Mill saw a "beautiful world" of hope. Through education he believed that the workers would come to realize the full impact of the Malthusian doctrine and would then voluntarily regulate their numbers. He maintained that workers could form cooperatives and unions and that they could seek higher wages. While generally opposed to government regulation and while recognizing the danger to the survival of individualism from a system of communism, he felt that legislation was the only way in which the children and women who worked in the factories could be protected. Consequently, by favoring government intervention when necessary to remedy injustices, Mill greatly modified the doctrine of "laissez faire." He called for inheritance taxes and the taxation of rents. His book was a great success, and in addition to the regular seven editions published, Mill, at his own expense, had a cheap one-volume edition printed so that his message of hope could reach the working class.

Commentary

John Stuart Mill is best known today for his contributions to political science and ethics. His essay, *On Liberty,* is perhaps the finest piece ever written on individualism and it is essentially a manifesto against despotism of all kinds. He was a peaceful and reasonable man who had only two loves — love for his wife and love for knowledge. He was above all an intellectual "par excellence." Consequently, while he called himself "a Socialist" later in life, his brand of socialism was a very mild one for he actually stood midway between capitalism and socialism.

Ironically, his economic message of hope for the peaceful improvement of society was published in the same year that a small pamphlet issued forth from a press in Belgium — a pamphlet which would bury all hope for the peaceful and evolutionary improvement of the lot of the workers. This pamphlet, under the title of *The Communist Manifesto,* would carry across the world Karl Marx's cry of revolutionary socialism.

CHAPTER VI

THE INEXORABLE WORLD OF KARL MARX

Summary
     The year 1848 dawned on a Europe in which socialism had so far been a minor factor in political and economic thought. The pessimism of Malthus and Ricardo was beginning to give way to the optimism of Mill, but the lot of the vast working class had not been greatly improved. The worker was still poorly paid and poorly housed and even in England — the most democratic of the European nations — he still did not have the right to vote. The peasant was still discriminated against by high prices and in many cases had been forced off the land. The government of France was controlled by bankers and businessmen, Italy was years away from unity and was dominated by Austria. A reactionary Prussia in which there was not even a parliament was also dominated by Austria, which was governed by the interests of arch-conservatism. Under Tsar Nicholas I, Russia was a frozen land of autocracy. Thus, the future held little promise for the masses.

And then in 1848 Europe was engulfed in a series of revolutions as revolts broke out in France, in Austria, Bohemia, and Hungary, in Prussia, and in Italy. The chief factors which led to them were those of nationalism, romanticism, and middle-class liberalism. All of them failed except in the case of France, and even there the aspirations for more democracy failed. They failed because they were spontaneous, unconnected uprisings which were led chiefly by poets and idealists rather than by hard-boiled practical politicians and statesmen. But amid the clamor a new voice had been heard — the voice of militant workers demanding the "right to work" — and a new type of socialism appeared in Europe. This was *Revolutionary Socialism.* All the unsuccessful uprisings had been suppressed by military force, with much flowing of blood — and none was more costly than the uprising in Paris where the workers staged the bloodiest street fighting in French history. Thus, the scene was ideally set for the appearance of *The Communist Manifesto*—written by Karl Marx with the collaboration of Friedrich Engels.

Karl Marx (1818-1883) was born in Germany, the second son of a liberal, middle-class Jewish family which later adopted Christianity. He was able to pursue a college education, but contrary to his father's wishes that he study law and follow him in that occupation, Marx soon transferred from the University of Bonn to Berlin University. There he dedicated himself to the study of philosophy and was particularly influenced by the ideas of Hegel. He then received his Ph.D. at the University of Jena in 1841. His ambition to become a professor was blocked by the authorities who objected to his well-known liberal views, which included a belief in constitutional government and in atheism. He then turned to journalism and became the editor of a radical newspaper which was soon suppressed because of his attacks on absolutism in government. It was at this time that Marx began to study socialist literature, soon becoming converted to socialism. He continued his journalistic career, going to Paris, then to Brussels, back to Paris, then back to Germany—each time managing to stay just one jump ahead of the authorities who took a dim view of his socialistic doctrines.

In Paris he had begun his close association with Engels—a friendship which was to last for the rest of Marx's life. Friedrich Engels was the son of a wealthy German textile manufacturer, but as devoted to socialist ideals as was Marx. In Brussels the two collaborated to produce *The Communist Manifesto,* which was to be the program of the "League of Communists" —a loose organization of discontented workers who desired fundamental political and economic changes. The result was *the first great pronouncement of modern socialism.* The term "Communist" was chosen to distinguish the League and its program from the socialist party of Louis Blanc in France, as well as from the "Utopian Socialists" for whom Marx only had contempt.

Wherever Marx went, he was active as an agitator, organizing workers' movements and editing communist papers. With the collapse of the European revolutions of 1848-1849, the established governments took steps to crush all signs of revolutionary activity and the Communist League was dissolved and its leaders thrown into jail. Marx fled to England in the summer of 1849, at the age of thirty-one, to spend the remainder of his life in London. There he, his wife (the beautiful daughter of a Prussian aristocrat), his children, and a faithful servant were to spend a miserable existence with abject poverty and near starvation their daily fare. His devoted wife was to see two of their children buried before she followed them to the grave after years of illness, with Marx unable to buy medicine and sufficient food, or to move out of the slum area in which they lived. Throughout, Marx was a devoted husband and father—affectionately called "The Moor" by his children. However, his only steady earned income was one guinea a week for his reports on European affairs to the *New York Tribune,* whose editor at the time was Charles A. Dana. At times he could not send his reports to New York because he did not have the money to pay for the postage, and on more than one occasion during a cold winter he pawned his shoes and his overcoat in order to buy bread and potatoes. What actually kept his family alive was the generous financial aid sent to him by Engels. Undoubtedly, these years of extreme poverty account for much of the bitterness evident in Marx's writings and in his relationships with those outside of his family. To add to his misery, he suffered greatly from boils.

All the while, Marx generally spent the hours from ten in the morning until seven at night each day in the British Museum library. Year after year he pored over the books and manuscripts available there on economics, gathering the enormous mass of data which was to form the basis of his *Das Kapital.* The book was over eighteen years in preparation, with the main part—volume I—finally being published in 1867 in Germany. Written in German, no English translation was available for twenty years. Ironically enough, the first translation into another language was a Russian edition of 1872—allowed by the official Russian censor on the ground that not many would read the book because of its difficult style and strictly scientific method of exposition.

Marx's life was not only one of poverty, but also one of disappointment. He did not live to see communism triumph anywhere but he did live to see the conditions of the working class materially improve, contrary to his dire predictions. His later life was filled with bickering with other socialists over the validity of his interpretations, with the course of the First International (an international workingmen's association of seven million members), and with his bitter feud with the anarchists, Proudhon and Bakunin. Finally one day, disgusted with all the arguments within the working-class movement, Marx declared, "I am not a Marxist," and not long after quietly died. At his death, only volume I of his masterpiece, *Das Kapital* (Capital) had been published. Volume II was published by Engels in 1885, volume III in 1894, and volume IV in 1910.

As Marx did not make a systematic presentation of his philosophy, it is necessary to discover his basic concepts from a study of *The Communist Manifesto* and *Das Kapital,* each of which was written for a different purpose. First, however, it is necessary to understand how Marx developed the principle of "dialectical materialism" from the dialectical method of the German philosopher, Hegel. Hegel's concept was that change occurred as the result of a synthesis of opposing forces. Thus, a given idea (Thesis) when challenged by a new and opposing idea (Antithesis) would result in a new concept (Synthesis) which was somewhat closer to the truth than the initial two ideas. In accepting this fundamental premise of Hegel, Marx was indebted to Hegelian dialectics but he went much further than had

Hegel. While Hegel had confined the dialectical method to the world of ideas, Marx maintained that it also applied to the world of reality. The thesis and antithesis became to Marx actual opposing forces existing in the universe, with a synthesis being the objective result which, becoming in its turn a new thesis with a new antithesis, led to the creation of a new objective synthesis. Consequently, Marx substituted realism for Hegel's idealism and went on to explain the history of the world and of all events on this basis — by what he called "inverted Hegelism," or "putting Hegel right side up" by stressing the reality of materialism. To Marxian socialism this was the greatest principle which Marx discovered — *"dialectical materialism,"* or as it is often called, the "Marxian dialect." This led to Marx's *economic interpretation of history,* or "historical materialism." But let *The Communist Manifesto* carry the message.

It opens with the declaration, "A spectre is haunting Europe — the spectre of Communism..." and closes with the ringing cry: "The Communists disdain to conceal their views and aims. They openly declare that their ends can be attained only by the forcible overthrow of all existing social conditions. Let the ruling classes tremble at a Communistic revolution. The proletarians have nothing to lose but their chains. They have a world to win. Working men of all countries, unite!"

It then brings in the economic interpretation of history and the concept of class struggle: "The history of all hitherto existing society is the history of class struggles. Freeman and slave, patrician and plebian, lord and serf, guildmaster and journeyman, in a word, oppressor and oppressed, stood in constant opposition to one another, carried on uninterrupted, a now hidden, now open fight, a fight that each time ended, either in a revolutionary reconstitution of society at large, or in the common ruin of the contending classes." This economic interpretation of history was further elaborated on by Engels: "...human beings must have food and drink, clothing and shelter, first of all, before they can interest themselves in politics, science, art, religion and the like." In brief, the struggle for food, clothing and shelter are all-important, determining everything else in human affairs. The history of mankind, then, according to Marx, is primarily the story of the exploitation of one class by another. In prehistoric ages, there was a tribal or classless type of society, but in historic times, classes have developed, and the masses of the human population had become, first, slaves, then serfs in the feudal era, and next, property-less wage slaves in the capitalistic era. Applying the theory of dialectical materialism, the *"inevitable"* next step was to be a revolt of the workers which would overthrow the ruling capitalist class and establish a "dictatorship of the proletariat," to be followed by communal ownership and a return to a classless social organization.

As to the historic role of the proletariat, the *Manifesto* argues: "All previous historical movements were movements of minorities, or in the interest of minorities. The proletariat movement is the self-conscious, independent movement of the immense majority." Where do the Communists come in? Why, they are to be the intellectual elite of the proletariat group, their role to direct and represent the interests of the revolutionary movement as a whole during the class struggle. Their immediate aim is the same as that of all the other proletariat parties in every country — "...formation of the proletariat into a class, overthrow of the bourgeois of supremacy, conquest of political power by the proletariat." The final result then, will be the abolition of all classes — a classless society — with the guiding principle to be, "From each according to his abilities, to each according to his needs."

While *The Communist Manifesto* clearly states the revolutionary aims of Communism and maintains that capitalism must inevitably destroy itself, *Das Kapital* is Marx's analysis of just why and how capitalism will destroy itself. It is a critique of political economy and attempts to explain economics in an objective, coldly analytical, and "scientific" manner. To Marx, his "scientific" arguments were irrefutable, and therefore, *Das Kapital* was prognosticating the doom of capitalism.

Marx sets the scene for his attack on capitalism by describing a capitalistic world of perfect competiton — where competition is free, without any monopolies or unions. Every product there sells for exactly its correct price — which is its value. Agreeing with Adam Smith and David Ricardo on the definition of "value," Marx states that the value of a product is the amount of labor which goes into making it. The worker wishes to sell his labor-power, and the capitalist wishes to make profits. But how can there be any profits if everything sells for its exact value? It would be simple for profits to arise if there were monopolies to set excessive prices, or if the capitalists were to pay labor less than what it is worth — but Marx has chosen the most difficult example of capitalism to describe, that of perfect competition. He has done this deliberately because if he can show that capitalism in its most perfect form — that "wonderful world of Adam Smith" — is unworkable, then there is no possible chance for the survival of the actual world of capitalism, with its monopolies and imperfections.

Das Kapital goes on to explain that in the hypothetical world of pure competition profits do arise. They arise from the one product or commodity which is distinctive — labor-power. How? Well, the worker sells his labor-power to the capitalist for exactly what it is worth — its value. Its value is worth exactly what it takes to make it — in other words, what it takes to keep the laborer alive. So here Marx agrees with Ricardo that the wage of labor is its subsistence wage. Now comes his explanation of the existence of profits. While the actual value of labor is equal to the labor it takes to keep him alive — which takes the form of his actual wages — the worker actually *produces more* than this for the capitalist. How? By working extra hours. Suppose that what it takes to keep a worker alive is equal to six hours of labor. If labor is priced at $1 an hour, then the actual value of the worker's labor is $6 for the six hours worked. However, the worker is not hired to work just six hours a day — he works the regular *work-day,* which in Marx's time was ten or twelve hours, and which today is eight hours. So the worker's daily production is actually worth $10 or $12, says Marx, while the capitalist is only paying him $6 — his subsistence wage. The difference is *"surplus value"* and gives rise to the capitalist's profits. In short, while the worker is only paid a daily wage equal to his subsistence requirements, his actual production for the entire work-day results in extra units of products, and their value — "surplus value" — is translated into profits for the capitalist when he sells the extra units at the regular selling price. The capitalist has "stolen" what is rightfully the worker's. This theory of "surplus value" was Marx's second most important contribution to Marxian socialism.

How can such a thing occur? Simple, answers Marx. It is because the capitalist has a monopoly on the means of production and can therefore force the worker to work a full day if he wants a job. Since the typical factory work-week in England during Marx's time of writing averaged slightly better than eighty hours, his concept of "surplus value" was not as far-fetched as it seems today under different working conditions.

Continuing with Marx's analysis, the capitalist continually strives to obtain more and more "surplus value" by expanding his production, thereby increasing his profits. However, he is in competition with other capitalists, and they are doing the same thing. As all strive to increase production they hire more workers, which means that the capitalists bid against each other and consequently push wages up — which results in the decrease of their profits. So they face the same problem which confronted Smith's and Ricardo's capitalists — how to avoid the disappearance of their profits. Ricardo had solved this problem by his "Iron Law of Wages" — the theory that workers would increase their supply through increased offspring — and so had Smith with his "Law of Population" which did not extend to Ricardo's pessimistic conclusion. But Marx rejects this solution because he views the workers favorably — as being too enlightened to continue increasing their offspring. At the same time he scornfully rejects the Malthusian Doctrine, labeling it "a libel on the human race." Instead, he sees the capitalist providing his own solution through the adoption of labor-saving machinery. By substituting machinery, the capitalist forces more and more workers out of their jobs, thus increasing the labor supply — which means a decrease in wages. So while his solution differs from Smith's and Ricardo's, the result is the same — a pushing down of wages.

However, the solution is not a real solution for the capitalist's problem after all, continues Marx, for as the capitalist adds machines he has to pay the full value price for them — their actual yield value. Consequently, he cannot realize any "surplus value" from them — as he formerly could from human labor. He is therefore defeating his own purpose, but he is forced to do so because his competitors are adding machines to increase their production. As everyone adds more and more machines, the percentage of profits steadily falls until the point is reached where production is no longer profitable. Bankruptcies result and the smaller firms are forced out of business.

But as more and more workers lose their jobs, labor is forced to accept lower wages. Machines are dumped, human labor is hired by the remaining firms and for awhile "surplus value" — and profits — returns. Not for long, however, as this is a vicious cycle which Marx portrays, for the increase in hiring of workers leads to increased wages, which leads to decreased profits, which leads to increased use of machines, which leads to the loss of "surplus value," etc., etc. All the while, however, the contrast between the working class and the capitalistic class is growing sharper and sharper, with their respective interests further and further apart. And here the capitalists are "their own grave diggers," for on one hand the working class, increasingly dissatisfied with its increasing misery, is growing larger and larger — while on the other hand, the capitalistic class is getting smaller and smaller as the larger capitalists gobble up their smaller and weaker competitors. In the process, the capitalists have forced the disappearance of the middle class, and now there are only two classes — the proletariat class of workers, and the capitalists. The remaining large capitalists begin to "dump" their excess goods abroad and capitalism becomes imperialistic, with the result that the working class now shares its misery all over the world. When finally there remains only a few great capitalists, with vast masses of increasingly hostile workers facing them, the time will have come for the proletariat to rise and sweep away the capitalists — "The expropriators are expropriated." That is the message of *Das Kapital*. Capitalism, being unworkable, finally puts itself into the position where it is destroyed.

Marx then looked at the real capitalistic world of imperfect competition and predicted the trends which capitalism would follow in the future. These predictions he called the *"laws of motion"* — and surprisingly, most of them have come true.

First, as the economy expanded, profits would fall — both within the business cycle, and outside of it. (This is partly true, as profits do tend to fall within the business cycle. However, they do not fall as a steady downward trend outside of the business cycle, but have instead risen.)

Second, as profits fall, business would ceaselessly seek new techniques in order to survive, by innovating, inventing, and experimenting. (This is true, as is seen today from the definite trend toward diversification.)

Third, there would be business cycles of depression and boom. (Very true.)

Fourth, huge firms would come to dominate the business scene. (Very true.)

Finally, capitalism would disappear. (This of course has not come to pass. However, it has come to pass in Russia, in Eastern Europe, and in China. In Western Europe it has partly disappeared, or at least been greatly modified—even in that bastion of "laissez faire," Great Britain. In fact, capitalism has largely failed everywhere except in the United States. The failure has not been due primarily to economic reasons, but to social reasons—but Marx predicted this too by asserting that the special interests of absolutist governments would prevent any efforts at corrective legislation for the worst evils of the capitalistic system.)

Commentary

A certain amount of commentary has already been given along with the summary of this chapter, as Marx is difficult enough to understand. The distinguishing characteristic of Marx's vision of the future lies in the word, "inexorable." It means "inflexible," "relentless." So to Marx, his description of future events was as inflexible as the law of gravitation, and events would move relentlessly in the direction which he portrayed.

However, contrary to Marx's predictions, the destruction of capitalism has not yet come about, and the lot of the working class has steadily improved. Further, in no case where Communism has triumphed has the revolution taken place in an industrial nation. Russia, China, and Cuba were all primarily agricultural nations when the revolutions occurred. So were the "satellite" nations of eastern Europe—with the exception of Czechoslovakia (which is really in central Europe)—and they were all taken over at a time of war, from without. Yugoslavia was primarily agricultural, and the disappearance of capitalism there took place during wartime. Spain and Greece, which almost became communistic, were also agricultural. On the other hand, Germany and Italy, while not being communistic, were largely prevented from becoming so by fascism—in which state capitalism became a working partner with private capitalism. What countries did become communistic did so not as the result of Marx's predictions but largely as the result of the work of the professional revolutionaries—a small highly-disciplined minority group following the "active revolutionaries" concept of Lenin. Further, even Lenin made a compromise with capitalism after attaining power in Russia (N.E.P.), and the Soviet Union today has adopted certain capitalistic practices.

Yet, one cannot deny the tremendous impact of Karl Marx, and no Communist nation or party anywhere fails to pay homage to his teachings. Non-communist economists find the weakest point in *Das Kapital* to be the theory of "surplus value," for it does not satisfactorily explain prices and these economists do not accept labor as being the measure of "value." On the other hand, economists have not come up with any other agreed-upon measure of value. Liberals and humanitarians cannot accept Marx's economic interpretation of history, for they deny that all historical developments have been determined purely by economic considerations, with the denial of the importance of such other factors as religion, nationalism, and human personality. Thus, in the Marxian world the "Hero" has a subordinate role in the motivation of historical events. On the other hand, until the time of Marx, the effect of economics in human affairs had been all but over-looked by historians.

While capitalism has not been swept away, as Marx predicted, socialism has been on the rise throughout the world ever since his time, and communism is a form of socialism — though an unyielding, inexorable variety. In the United States socialism has been avoided largely as the result of government anti-trust legislation and regulation of public utilities — measures which were not anti-capitalist but anti-monopoly, so that competitive capitalism could more freely survive. Practically all western European countries practice mixed elements of socialism and capitalism, as indeed does the United States. Throughout the world today, from the impoverished nations of Latin America to the emerging nations of Africa and Asia, the communist banner of Karl Marx is unfurled — proof of the fact that his concepts cannot be lightly dismissed, and that he is entitled to be called: "Prophet of the Proletariat."

A few terms should be clarified:

Marxism
The gospel of Communism according to Karl Marx, incorporating dialectical materialism. While a plain Communist may believe in the final goal of communism without asserting that it will come about exactly as Marx predicted, the Marxist brand of communism accepts Marx's every word and explanation as essentially true. Thus, a "deviationist" would be one who deviated to any extent from Marx's teachings. Both forms of communism accept the concept of "revolutionary socialism" — the attainment of the communistic society by violent and bloody revolution, if necessary, as opposed to the peaceful and democratic methods of the Socialists. In terms of being "left" or "right," the Marxists are further "left" than the Communists, who in turn are to the "left" of the Socialists.

Scientific Socialism
What Marx and Engels called their ideas, as expressed in The Communist Manifesto and Das Kapital, termed "scientific laws" which explained the economic determination of history, the class struggle, and the inevitable downfall of capitalism with the triumph of the proletariat class.

Capitalists
The class which provides or controls the capital for the production of goods; also called the "haute bourgeoisie."

Bourgeoisie

The middle class, technically divided between the rich capitalists ("haute bourgeoisie") and the small shopkeepers, government officials, lawyers, doctors, independent farmers, and teachers (all grouped together as the "petite bourgeoisie"). A term generally used by the Marxists to describe people with private property. "Bourgeois" is the usual spelling for use as an adjective.

Proletariat

The class of lowly wage earners; the workers.

Anarchism

The belief that all forms of government are oppressive. The anarchists were not content to wait for the communistic "withering away" of the state —they believed in ending government rule everywhere by assassinating public officials. The early modern theorist of the benefits of anarchism was William Godwin, whose *Political Justice* (1793) expressed a utopian ideal. The "Father of Anarchism," however, is considered to be Pierre Proudhon (1809-1865) who quarreled violently with Marx, and whose book, *What is Property?* answered the question in the title by stating that "Property is theft." The anarchist who championed direct action by using "the bomb and the revolver" was the Russian, Mikhail Bakunin, who was originally a Marxist but who broke with Marx and became his bitter enemy. The anarchists are at the extreme "left" of all political groups.

CHAPTER VII

THE VICTORIAN WORLD AND THE UNDERWORLD OF ECONOMICS

Summary

The prediction of Karl Marx that the working class would suffer increasing misery did not come to pass during the Victorian Age (the reign of Queen Victoria, 1837-1901), for wages climbed upward while the working day grew shorter. Even Marx and Engels were forced to admit that the English proletariat was becoming more and more bourgeois. This was because the Victorian world was one of prosperity and optimism. That optimism was officially expressed by the recognized economists of the day, an increasing number of whom were respected professors. Consequently, Marx was dismissed by the orthodox economists as at best a "crank," and his theories confined to the "underworld of economics." This was the proper phrase to describe the place in the Victorian world for all "cranks" and non-conformists whose concepts had won neither acceptance nor respectability. And this was the resting place not only for Marx, for the pessimistic Malthus, and the "ridiculous" Utopians, but also for three of the following five economists of the Victorian Age.

FRANCIS Y. EDGEWORTH

Edgeworth, a shy and retiring professor, was a brilliant scholar. Becoming interested in the subject of economics because it dealt with quantities, he applied mathematics to economics and came up with his *Mathematical Psychics* (1881). Its thesis was that "every man is a pleasure-machine," and this was based on mathematical formulas. Of course, some men — those with skill and talent — were better "pleasure-machines" than others, and men in general were better "pleasure-machines" than women. In developing his theme, Edgeworth justified the divisions of sex and status which were apparent in the world, and he took a dim view of the future of trade-unions, considering them to be "imperfections."

What was unique about Edgeworth was that he "proved" all his contentions on the basis of mathematical formulas. Essentially, he was a conservative, and he defended this philosophy through the use of long, complicated algebraic expressions. Being an English conservative, he won a following in the conservative Victorian world and his book was an immediate success. While perhaps of some value in focusing attention on the possibilities of the use of mathematics as an aid to economics, much of what Edgeworth developed was ridiculous. His weakness was in ignoring the human factor, but it is a revealing insight into the nature of the Victorian Age to learn that his thesis was *not* banished to the "underworld" but given recognition.

FREDERIC BASTIAT

In sharp contrast to Edgeworth was the French wit, Bastiat, who heaped ridicule on the economic policies of his age. Living from 1801 to 1850, he added the deft touch of humor to the subject of economics. In his book, *Economic Sophisms,* he attacked the Socialists and defended free trade, but his special attacks were directed against the protective tariff. Beneath his wit lay the truth of his criticism — but in the Victorian world he was easily cast into the "underworld."

HENRY GEORGE (1839-1897)

With Henry George, the "underworld of economics" gained an American recruit — a rugged individual whose experiences in life had included the following vocations: adventurer, gold prospector, worker, sailor, publisher, journalist, lecturer, government bureaucrat, "tramp," and politician. Unlike his fellow dwellers of the "underworld," during his lifetime he was extremely popular — much more so in England than in his native United States. An active fighter for his beliefs, he was almost elected mayor of New York City, barely losing to the candidate of the Tammany Hall machine and running ahead of Theodore Roosevelt. Drafted to run a second time, he died on election eve.

His contribution to economics was the passionately written book, *Progress and Poverty* (1879). Its thesis was that the true cause of poverty was land rent. To Henry George it was the height of injustice that men should enjoy fabulous incomes merely from the fact that they owned land, while not contributing any real services to their society. Not only did rent work a hardship on the capitalist—as Ricardo had maintained—but it was also detrimental to the worker. Worst of all, said George, rent was the cause of depressions. But part of his thesis was *the solution* which he proposed: *a Single Tax on land,* equal to the rental and thus wiping out rent. With this one Single Tax, all other taxes could be eliminated and this would lead to increased wages and increased capital earnings, for more money would be free to circulate with no taxes for the non-landowner to pay. In short, the Single Tax would be the panacea ("cure-all") for society.

Regardless of a possible lack of logic in George's message, his book became a best-seller and overnight he became famous. *Progress and Poverty* was praised as a worthy successor to the famous *Wealth of Nations,* and George won an international reputation after a lecture tour to England. The Single Tax became an obsession with him and he formed "Land and Labor Clubs," filled with enthusiastic members. His book sold more copies than all the economic texts previously published in the United States, and even today there is an active loyal following. However, the official world of economics had nothing but contempt for his ideas—so Henry George was also exiled to the "underworld of economics."

JOHN A. HOBSON (1858-1940)

Of far more importance than the theories of Bastiat and Henry George was the theme which occupied the attention of the third economic "heretic." The theme was imperialism, for the Victorian Age was also the age of Imperialism—the time when Great Britain, France, Germany, Belgium, Portugal, Holland, Italy, and Russia grabbed off colonies and economic concessions in Africa and Asia. The spirit of imperialism had swept through the Western world, including the United States. Between the Napoleonic Wars and 1870, the "laissez faire" doctrine of free trade was dominant and there was comparatively little interest shown in colonial expansion. From 1870 onward, however, came a drastic change in attitude and policy —motivated by various factors, such as the population pressure in Europe, the desire for military bases, and nationalism. However, the main driving force came from the economic factor, as the full effects of the Industrial Revolution swept throughout Europe. The result was that in the Victorian world imperialism became an extremely popular policy with virtually all classes of society, and its "virtues" were praised by its chief spokesman, Rudyard Kipling.

This, then, was the setting for the appearance of a timid scholar, John A. Hobson, who took a most critical look at the capitalistic world about him, and at imperialism in particular. He began by adopting the humanistic viewpoint of John Ruskin toward economics—a concept which stressed human values rather than cold statistics. Next, by becoming the co-author of an economic treatise which suggested that savings might lead to depression and unemployment, he lost favor with the orthodox economists and was banished from participating in the London University Extension Lectures. As a result, he became a social critic and began to examine the leading questions of the day. The chief topic for conversation in England was Africa, where the Boer War between the Dutch colonists and the English over control of South Africa was brewing. Hobson made a personal trip to Africa and his research there convinced him that his warning of the results of oversaving was justified. Returning to England, he quietly prepared his major work, in which the effects of savings and imperialism were combined to form his thesis. In 1902, with the effect of a bomb, his book, *Imperialism, a Study,* appeared.

It was the most devastating attack ever made on the capitalistic system and on the philosophy of imperialism. While being a non-Marxist, Hobson went even further than had Karl Marx. While Marx had only predicted that capitalism would destroy itself, *Hobson's thesis* was that *imperialism becomes the road to war*—leading to the possible destruction of the whole world as a consequence. Basically, his argument is as follows. Capitalism has an insolvable problem—the fact that the rich get richer and the poor get poorer. As the result of this vast inequality in the distribution of income, capitalism finds itself in the situation where neither the rich nor the poor can consume enough goods produced. The rich are few in number and they can only consume so much. The poor, while large in number, do not have sufficient income to consume much. What happens then is that the rich—both individuals and corporations—are forced to put the bulk of their income into savings. Savings are of no benefit unless they are put to use—into further production of goods—as otherwise, purchasing power dries up. But where is the market for more goods when there are already too many goods, due to the inability of both rich and poor to consume enough?

Here Hobson brings in imperialism, for the only obvious answer is to invest overseas, putting the savings to use. This is the solution—foreign investments to take off the excess of capital saved, and foreign markets to use the excess of goods produced. This, then, says Hobson, is *the reason for modern imperialism.* It is thus *created by the capitalistic system.* But dire consequences lie ahead. All capitalistic nations have the same problem—so they race each other to partition off the world, with each nation trying to grab the biggest slice. This means bitter competition and rivalry—and war becomes probable.

Needless to say, Hobson's indictment of capitalism hardly made a dent in the official economic thought of the Victorian world, and he was sent to join Bastiat and Henry George who had already preceded him to the "underworld of economics." However, from one quarter there came a warm response. A certain Russian exile read Hobson's work and appropriated his thesis, adding to it and wrapping it all up in a glittering package, *Imperialism, the Highest Stage of Capitalism,* which was published in 1916. The author was Vladimar Ilich Ulyanov — Lenin. There was a great difference. Hobson did not look with favor on communism, and his book was a keen analysis of capitalism and imperialism, based on logic and devoid of any class favoritism. And Hobson did not make a dogma of his thesis. He was frankly puzzled because throughout history there had been periods when capitalism had shown little interest in imperialism. Further, while his thesis was indeed that imperialism becomes the road to war, he did not maintain that it would inevitably lead to war. The tendency was there, even the probability — but not the certainty.

On the other hand, with Lenin the probability of war became a certainty, and capitalism and imperialism were woven together to fit in beautifully with Marxist dogma. Marx's prediction of the doom of capitalism was carried further, to show that imperialism was the last stage to be reached by capitalism before it died. It was the final stage of decay of the system. And this was the view of Stalin — and is the view today of the Communists. So it is that the official Communist line charges that all United States interests in the underdeveloped countries of the world — whether that interest is shown by corporations or by such projects as "Point Four" and the Peace Corps — is actually motivated by design and is representative of imperialism.

The United States reply to this charge is that foreign investment and foreign trade alone do not represent imperialism, for there must also be political interference and economic exploitation of those countries before you have a case of imperialism. In fact, modern U.S. investment practices show quite the contrary — as for example, the case of Standard Oil Company in Venezuela where 50% of the company's profits are returned to the Venezuelan economy, and where Standard Oil is training native administrators who will one day take over the management of the company. In short, the United States defense is that there is a world of difference between profits and plunder — and the best example of a powerful country plundering a weaker is given by the Soviet Union itself.

Commentary

"Imperialism" refers to the extension of authority or control — whether direct or indirect — of one people over another. In this sense, imperialism is as old as the history of mankind. During the ancient history of our Western civilization, Greece and Rome furnished good examples. In modern history, the Age of Discovery ushered in a period when the nation-states of Europe raced to stake out colonies and to monopolize overseas trade. Portugal, Spain, Holland, France, and England were the examples. The result was the acute rivalry which helped to bring on the great colonial wars which began in the early part of the eighteenth century and which did not end until the close of the Napoleonic Wars. Then interest weakened as the doctrine of "laissez faire" replaced that of Mercantilism.

A new period of imperialism—referred to as the "new" imperialism, or *"economic imperialism"* took place from 1870 to 1914. This is known as "Europe's Golden Age of Imperialism." It was motivated by the effects of the Industrial Revolution and characterized by the economic and political domination of underdeveloped countries by powerful modern nations. The stress was given to the economic advantages. Western Europe—which controlled most of the world's finance, commerce, military power, and intellectual life—extended its power over the peoples of Asia and Africa. The entire continent of Africa was so partitioned that only two independent nations remained by 1914—Ethiopia and Liberia. Asia was a fertile hunting ground for the European nations and vast but weak China soon became known as "a ripe Melon" to be carved up. These are the historical facts. By 1914 some 283 million whites directly controlled over 900 million non-Europeans, mostly in Africa and Asia. And this staking out of colonies and economic "spheres of influence" did lead to bitter rivalry among the European nations, and was a strong factor leading to the outbreak of World War I—demonstrated by the fact that the terms of peace stripped Germany of every one of her colonies.

The basic question raised by Hobson was whether this stage of imperialism—"economic imperialism"—was inseparably related to capitalism. In other words, do capitalism and imperialism naturally go together. The Communists charge that they do. The United States and Western Europe say that they do not. The developments today are of course far different, for practically every one of the former imperialistic holdings have been lost to the colonial powers. At the height of imperialism, 5/6 of the world was weak, needy, and defenseless, while the remaining 1/6 was rich and powerful. Today, the poor 5/6 is still poor, but it is independent and defiantly aggressive. The formerly rich 1/6 is still rich, but on the defensive. The all-important question now is whether the defiantly aggressive majority in the world will be swayed by the Marxist dogma which has adapted Hobson's thesis.

It is for this reason that John A. Hobson, while ignored in his day, was the most profound of all the economic thinkers discussed in this chapter.

ALFRED MARSHALL

Summary
Alfred Marshall was the most famous economist of the Victorian World. There was no question of this Englishman's "acceptance" and "respectability," for his *Principles of Economics* (1890) was a tremendous success and is still read by students of economics. His thesis was *"equilibrium"*—the self-adjusting and self-correcting nature of the economic world, and the foundation of his economics was the concept of *time*. There was the short-run period of time, and the long-run period of time to consider. For instance, both had to be considered in answering the question of

whether diamonds are expensive because of the production costs and efforts involved in obtaining them, or because of the demand for them by people who like to wear them. In the short-run, explained Marshall, it is the demand which makes them expensive, but in the long-run, it is the costs of production.

In the determination of price, supply and demand were equally important — as equally important as are the two blades of a pair of scissors in cutting. To Marshall, *economics* was *"an engine for the discovery of truth"* — the "truth" being the cause and cure of poverty. He built up an elaborate system of economics which delighted established thought and which satisfied the businessman, and his system has been incorporated into the economic principles which are taught today in all introductory economic courses in England and the United States. His most brilliant pupil was John Maynard Keynes, who was to make a much larger splash in the world of economic thought.

Yet, brilliant as Marshall was, nothing that he said went far enough. The "time" which he wrote so much about was an *abstract* time, and his world of economics was a world of economic theory. And those theories were — and still are — hopelessly unrelated to the very real and practical world of economic and social events.

CHAPTER VIII

THE SAVAGE WORLD OF THORNSTEIN VEBLEN

Summary
So the world of economics had for its official spokesmen the conservative professional economists of Europe. However, as the full effects of the Industrial Revolution spread from Europe to America, the free enterprise atmosphere of the United States became a far different thing than the European practice of "laissez faire." In contrast to the European scene, the game of making money in the United States was a rough and *savage* affair, devoid of all sportsmanship. The rapier of the gentleman gave way to the brass knuckles of the roughneck. In the United States any man could prove his worth through business success, regardless of his ancestors, and *money* became the passport for entrance into the upper classes. Men such as William H. Vanderbilt (worthy heir to his "Commodore" father), John D. Rockefeller, Jay Gould, Jim Fisk, and J. P. Morgan were each dedicated to ruining all competitors who might cross their respective paths. No quarter was asked, and the choice of weapons included dynamite as well as guns, with even kidnapping resorted to. In their dealings with the public, these "robber barons" were guided by William H. Vanderbilt's philosophy of "The public be damned."

Dishonesty was a virtue, the investor was a gullible fool, and the stock market a private casino for them to play while the public financed it all.

Such was the prevailing sentiment of the financial capitalists as Big Business in the United States made its amazing gains from 1865 through the early part of the twentieth century. A practical demonstration was the purchase of Anaconda Copper Company by William Rockefeller and Henry Rogers without the investment of a cent of their own—resulting in a gross profit to themselves of $36,000,000. The official economists viewed this scene unperturbed, their thoughts wrapped up with such terms as "enterprise," "thrift and accumulation," and "consumption." At best, they were only slightly apologetic, and they shared the common defect of blindness. They were too close to the actual scene to realize what was happening—too close to view things objectively. What was needed was a disinterested, detached view by an aloof observer—the objective view of a "foreigner." Such a need was admirably—and shockingly—filled by that most aloof of all skeptics, Thornstein Veblen.

Thornstein Veblen (1857-1929), born of immigrant Norwegians in Wisconsin, grew up in a pioneer Norwegian community in Minnesota. The drab farm life there was reflected in his austere childhood by such family beliefs that sugar and coffee were to be avoided as luxuries. He grew up remote and aloof, a strange man who was enigmatic but not a radical, and whose chief pattern of behavior was that of *non-conformity*. At the age of seventeen he was sent to an extremely religious Lutheran college—where he promptly threw the faculty into an uproar when it came his turn during the regular weekly meeting to suggest a way of converting the heathen. His suggestion was, "A Plea for Cannibalism." Meeting the niece of the president of the college, he promptly converted her to agnosticism. Several years later they were married.

Bad luck seemed to tag after him for he met with no immediate success in his plan to become a teacher. His first job lasted a year—until the academy closed. He went to Johns Hopkins where he expected a scholarship—which never materialized. Then he transferred to Yale where he received his Ph.D. in 1884. After that he returned home—to read and to loaf. He buried himself in works on political science, economics, sociology, anthropology—reading everything he could get his hands on. By normal standards he was lazy, for he refused to make up his bed every day (seeing no point in it), and he had the habit of using every dish in the kitchen, allowing them to accumulate in the sink until all were dirty. Not until then would he wash them—bringing in the hose to do so. His eccentricity extended to the use of the telephone—which he refused to put in, even in later life. This isolation from society continued for seven years, until at the age of thirty-four the family decided that he should resume graduate studies and attempt once more to enter into the academic field.

He appeared at Cornell in 1891 and when he walked into the office of the head of the economics department he must have shocked that conservative gentleman — for he was wearing corduroy pants and a coonskin cap. However, his learned mind impressed the older man for he was given a fellowship. The following year he accompanied the head of the department when the latter moved to the University of Chicago. At the University of Chicago, now thirty-five, and with the impressive salary of $520 *a year,* Veblen soon earned quite a reputation with his students. He refused to take class roll seriously and he assigned the grade of "C" to all his students — although he gladly changed the "C" to an "A" when a student needed it to qualify for a scholarship. He felt quite frankly that there were too many students, and the fewer that he had, the better. Nevertheless, and in spite of the fact that he mumbled and rambled in his lectures, his immense knowledge and his amazing mind made him an impressive scholar. By 1903 his salary had risen to the astonishing figure of $1,000 a year, and altogether he spent fourteen years at Chicago.

Meanwhile, it had become apparent that Veblen possessed an unusual fascination for women — which was fully reciprocated. He seemed to be always engaged in an affair — especially after his marriage — and when he made a trip to Europe with another woman, he was forced to look for employment elsewhere. His wife, incidentally, finally divorced him after twenty-three years of this kind of life. From Chicago Veblen went to Stanford, then to the University of Missouri, remarried, and finally retired at the age of seventy. He chose to live alone in a small cabin in the West where he could meditate without any distractions. There, aloof from his society, he died.

While his personal life was not a successful one, Veblen established a national reputation in the academic world as the result of two major books and a series of essays. His first book, *The Theory of the Leisure Class,* was published in 1899 when Veblen was forty-two. It was an overnight success, and the book for which he is best remembered. Its success was due primarily to the fact that most readers took it to be a satire of aristocracy and of the weaknesses of the rich. It was much more than that. Veblen's greatest contribution to knowledge was his refusal to accept the basic assumptions underlying classical economic thought. While the orthodox American economists had accepted the teachings of their European masters, Veblen went to the very roots of things by trying to discover the true nature of the society in which he lived.

So *The Theory of the Leisure Class* was exactly what its title suggested — an examination into the theory of the leisure class, with an explanation of the nature of economic man and the meaning of leisure itself. While the established economists explained men's actions entirely by self-interest and competition, Veblen probed deeper. He doubted that self-interest was what held society together, and he was not at all certain that leisure was preferable to work. In fact, he found that a leisure class did not exist in such societies as those of the American Indian, the Ainus of Japan, or the bushman of Australia. *Everyone* there *worked* — not for profit, but because of *a natural pride in workmanship* and a common concern for the future welfare of their children.

But in studying other communities, such as the Polynesians, the ancient inhabitants of Iceland, and the shogunate system of feudal Japan, Veblen found a very different kind of society. Here there existed a leisure class, but it was not an idle leisure class. Instead, its members worked very hard at seizing their riches through force or cunning, without contributing anything to the actual production of wealth. What was significant was that they lived thusly with the full approval of their community. So to Veblen *this marked a fundamental change in the attitude of the savage toward work.* What had once been a natural pride in work had become degraded by *the transfer of approval to the plundering and predatory ways of the leisure class.* The classical economists had considered the desire for leisure to be inherent in human nature — but Veblen maintained that it was pride in working which had been inherent in human nature originally. As men then began to plunder, seizing booty and women, and as they began to be admired for their strength and cunning, approval was transferred from the once-honorable way of life to the spirit of plunder — and the leisure class gained respect. As societies had progressed in history, continued Veblen, the leisure class had changed its occupations and refined its methods, but its goal had remained the same — the accumulation of goods without productive work, but by seizure. As to the application of his findings to the United States, Veblen wrote: "...by heredity human nature still is, and must indefinitely continue to be, savage human nature." It was not for booty or for women that the contemporary leisure class plundered, but for the accumulation of money and the lavish display of it. The savage had displayed his numerous wives, the barbarian his conquests of war — and in the same vein, modern man displayed his wealth.

So Veblen arrived at his thesis: that the leisure class advertised its superiority through *conspicuous consumption* — enjoying that leisure more fully by being able to display it before the eyes of the public. Thus, the modern U.S. businessman by seeking money and the accumulation of it, and then displaying it — sometimes subtly, but more often conspicuously — was the modern-day counterpart of his savage heritage. Further, everyone — the worker, the middle-class citizen, and the capitalist — sought through the conspicuous expenditure of money (even through its conspicuous waste at times) to prove his status. Carrying this theme a step farther, Veblen was able to explain why a proletariat revolution as predicted by Marx had not occurred in the United States. It was simply that the workers did not seek to overthrow the upper class, but rather strove to become part of that class themselves, by climbing into it. This explained *the social stability* of the nation.

In evaluating Veblen's thesis, much can be said for his view. Physical work in the United States is generally looked down upon, as compared with office work, and the prestige of the executive and the financier is very high. Business executives do continue to accumulate money well beyond normal needs and wants. As to conspicuous consumption, the modern-day term is "status symbol" — and a glance at the advertisements carried throughout the mass media shows the relevancy of this concept.

Veblen's *The Theory of Business Enterprise,* published in 1904, was essentially his own concept of the businessman in the present stage of capitalism. As such, it contained a shocking thesis, but the book did not make anything like the splash which his treatment of the leisure class had. This was because there was no mistaking of Veblen's description of the business world as being merely satire, and consequently, only the economists and scholars read it.

Breaking completely away from the view held by every economist since Adam Smith that the capitalist was the driving force behind economic progress, Veblen charged that the businessman was the *saboteur* of business! How could this possibly be? Very simple, explained Veblen. Society was now dominated by *the machine,* and the machine cared nothing about profits. Its only concern was for the accurate and regular performance of the function of production of goods. The businessman was therefore no longer needed — eliminated by the machine — and his former position of direction of economic production was now occupied by technicans and engineers. The businessman, however, as a member of the leisure class was still acutely interested in the accumulation of profits. How could he continue to make profits? His only opportunity in the machine age was by causing breakdowns in the regular flow of production so that values would fluctuate. Being on the "inside," he could then make a profit during the confusion which resulted. So the businessman cunningly built up credits, loans, and artificially-high capitalizations. Unfortunately, in the process the efficiency of the productive operations of society was continuously upset.

Looking to the future, Veblen predicted the end of the capitalist — brought about not by Marx's proletariat but by a much more powerful foe, the machine. The recurring business crisis brought about by the businessman would show to all the inability of the system to adjust itself. As the alternative, Veblen in his later writings hoped for the day when a corps of *engineers would take over the running of the economy,* along the lines of a huge, well-ordered production machine. And if this did not come to pass? Then eventually the plundering spirit of Big Business would increase until the system gave way to fascism.

There is a curious similarity between Veblen's general approach in his *Theory of Business Enterprise* and Saint-Simon's utopian concept of economic government. As to Veblen's thesis, it is rather extreme but it was applicable to the practices of the "robber barons" of his day. Those leaders of the business world were not at all interested in producing goods but in producing profits for themselves. A very good example of artificially-high capitalization was the founding of the United States Steel Corporation in 1901. Against real assets of some $682 million dollars, almost twice that amount of stocks and bonds were issued—at a capitalization cost of 150 million dollars, all of which was paid for by the investing public. So there was more than just a little justification for Veblen's scornful view of the American businessman. However, he greatly underestimated the ability of American democracy to correct these abuses.

Veblen continued his writings, but none of his books received the notices of his two "Theories." *Above all, he was a skeptic* as he probed into the problems of his society, and typical of this was his book, *Imperial Germany*. Although the book was so critical of Germany that the propaganda office of the U.S. government wanted to use it, the Post Office Department barred it from the mails because of its uncomplimentary observations on Great Britain and the United States. Veblen's *The Higher Learning in America,* published in 1918, was the most critical commentary ever directed to the American university. In it Veblen charged that the U.S. centers of learning had been transformed into centers of football and high-powered public relations. While certainly given to extremes, the value of Veblen lay in his pointing to anthropology and psychology as being better tools with which to study the society of man than the impersonal and theoretical "laws" of economics.

Commentary

Much reference has been made to the phrase, "robber barons," for indeed, Veblen's two major works formed a perfect description of their practices. The phrase, "robber barons" comes from the definitive and highly readable book, *The Robber Barons* (1934), written by Matthew Josephson. Also highly descriptive of the practices of the titans of Big Business during this period is Ida M. Tarbell's *History of the Standard Oil Company* (1903).

The "savage world" of Veblen was "savage" on two counts. First, the practices of the actual business world which he observed were savage. Secondly, in his examination into the nature of economic man, Veblen concluded that by heredity human nature was savage.

Thornstein Veblen has been pretty much ignored, officially. However, it is fair to note at least two things. In his book, *The Theory of the Leisure Class,* Veblen gave to common usage the term, "conspicuous consumption" and anticipated the rash of current writings on "status symbols." As to his second major work, *The Theory of Business Enterprise,* Veblen foreshadowed "Technocracy"—the belief in government by technical experts, with the use of "work units" of currency to be substituted for money. If alive today, Veblen would undoubtedly observe with a feeling of justification the latest trend in the development and use of computers and automation—the fact that not only are blue collar workers being dispossessed from their jobs by the machine through automation, but business executives are finding their positions increasingly occupied by computers.

CHAPTER IX

THE SICK WORLD OF JOHN MAYNARD KEYNES

Summary

Veblen had died in 1929 a few months before the "Great Crash"— when the values of stocks, which had reached an all-time high, came tumbling down. There had been no official warnings that such a financial catastrophe could possibly occur—in fact, quite the contrary. Prosperity was everywhere for all to see, and from President Hoover down to the lowly clerk, optimism was the keynote. In the United States there were 45 million jobs, a total income of 77 billion dollars, and the average American family was enjoying the highest standard of living ever experienced by any average family in all of history. Magazines featured articles on how everyone could become rich—the formula was to save a portion of earnings and invest it regularly in good common stocks. The public listened, and not only bankers and businessman, but barbers, bootblacks, and clerks rushed to place their orders on the stock market. It was very easy to do, for all could buy "on margin"—meaning that they could put down as little as 10% of the cost of the stock.

But beneath this surface of boom lay disturbing facts—disturbing that is, if they had not gone unnoticed. There were two million unemployed and banks were failing at the rate of 700 a year. Ominously, the distribution of income showed 24,000 families at the upper level of income, and some 6,000,000 families at the bottom level—an income ratio of 630 to 1. In this era of prosperity the average American family was mortgaged up to the hilt—unable to turn down the attraction of installment buying. Why not buy on installment when all this could be paid for quite easily from the expected high returns from buying stocks—bought on the installment plan too, of course. When the "Crash" came it caught the public, the titans of finance, the government officials, and the expert economists completely by surprise.

The stock market crash came in late October, and within two months the losses in stock values were awesome. Forty billion dollars of value had disappeared! And the downward trend continued. Fortunes were lost and suicides rose; nine million savings accounts vanished as banks failed by the thousands, and over 85,000 individual businesses were wiped out. Working girls worked for from 10c to 25c an hour, and breadlines formed in New York City alone at the rate of 2,000 men a day. The "Great Depression" was here. By 1933 the national income of the United States had dropped almost 50% and the average standard of living had declined to the level of twenty years earlier. There were at least 14,000,000 unemployed and the economy lay still like a fallen giant while a feeling of hopelessness swept the land. What no respectable economist had admitted could happen seemed to be a reality — *a permanent Depression.*

In such a situation, one would have expected a Marx to appear from the world of economic thought to attack with bitterness the plight of the unemployed and to offer a drastic solution. On the contrary, a solution was offered by a respectable Englishman, well-schooled in the theories of the orthodox economists. In fact, he had been the most brilliant pupil of the esteemed Alfred Marshall. Nevertheless, John Maynard Keynes, a brilliant intellectual, was adaptable enough in his outlook to make a very practical attempt to solve the problem of permanent Depression.

In contrast to Veblen, the life of John Maynard Keynes (1883-1946) was characterized by good fortune. Born into an old traditional English family he was able to attend the best schools. Reminiscent of the intellectual powers of John Stuart Mill was the fact that at the age of four Keynes was studying the meaning of interest. He won a scholarship to Eton, where he made superior grades and won numerous prizes. At King's College in Cambridge his grasp of economics was such that Marshall urged him to follow an academic career — which he declined as he had not yet made his fortune and was looking for a position more rewarding financially. He placed second in the civil service examinations for a position in the India Office of the government but found the work extremely displeasing. Resigning his position, he returned to Cambridge where he was made editor of the *Economic Journal* — England's most influential economic periodical — and he was to hold this position for the next thirty-three years. Keynes' chief trait was his ability to master so many diverse interests, for he was indeed the exception to the saying that "a jack of all trades is master of none." He was a great debater, expert bridge player, excellent mountain climber, connoisseur and collector of modern and classical art, an expert on currency and finance, and of course a renowned economist. In later life he became "Lord Keynes, Baron of Tilton," and while serving as a Director of the Bank of England also operated a theatre for profit.

His opportunity to gain a reputation came with World War I when he became a key figure in the Treasury and then was named delegate to the Paris Peace Conference of 1919. It was shortly after this that he made his fortune of over two million dollars — by spending half an hour in bed each day studying and speculating in the international markets.

Keynes attained national fame with the publication of his book, *The Economic Consequences of the Peace* (1919). His thesis was that the

Peace Treaties were unjust and could not work, with their apparent "solutions" ending in a fiasco. While this observation was also obvious to others, Keynes' view was the first one written which suggested a complete revision of the Treaties. The book was a great success, and international developments confirmed his thesis.

In 1930 appeared his *A Treatise on Money*, which was an attempt to explain how the whole economy operated and to particularly examine the problem of unexplained bursts of prosperity, followed by lows of depression. Earlier writers had attempted to explain this phenomenon by such theories as "mental disorders of the economy," and by the effect of sunspots but Keynes returned to the warning of Malthus—that the effect of savings could be the possible reason for depressions.

To understand this, it is necessary to understand what is meant by "prosperity" in the market economy. The true measure of the prosperity of a country is not its wealth in gold and silver, nor the total of its physical assets—it is in *its national income.* That national income is of course the total of all individual incomes in the country. The chief characteristic of income is its flowing movement—*income flows* from the pockets of people to the pockets of other people in their daily purchases and sales. Thus, this flowing—this movement—of income is largely a natural flowing arising from the use and *consumption of goods.* However, there is one part of income which does not flow in such daily transactions—Savings. So Savings represents that portion of income which is removed from the even flow of income. If that portion is completely withdrawn from use, by being hoarded or buried somewhere, it cannot be used. But no harm comes from the act of Savings in modern nations because Savings is usually put into banks or invested in stocks and bonds—becoming available for use by business when it wishes to expand its production by building more factories, adding more machinery, etc. When that happens, the money represented in Savings flows into the economy, and with the increased capacity for production more goods are produced—which means more jobs and greater prosperity. Depression arises from the situation occurring when Savings is not invested into expansion by business firms—for in that case, the portion of income withheld in the form of Savings remains idle and there is less income to flow.

This line of reasoning is known as *the "see-saw" theory of savings and investment*—a theory which was not original with Keynes but which he brilliantly explained. As a see-saw goes up and down, Savings (Thrift) goes up when Investment (Enterprise) goes down, and of course the reverse is true. In his polished examination of the "see-saw" theory, Keynes concluded that Depression was explained by a decline of Investment on one side, and the increased accumulation of Savings on the other. However, *Depression would only be temporary,* for with an abundant supply of Savings, interest rates would go down—leading to the flow of Savings into the higher rate of return to be gained from Investment for capital expansion. Thus, Prosperity would return.

Unfortunately, the "see-saw" theory had one shortcoming — its failure to explain a prolonged Depression, such as the Great Depression of the 1930's. While the rate of interest at that time declined, no upswing of Investment took place. The see-saw didn't move — the economy remained paralyzed in Depression. Recognizing this shortcoming, Keynes pondered over the problem and developed *a revolutionary solution in his masterpiece, The General Theory of Employment, Interest, and Money,* published in 1936.

Keynes made the following pessimistic diagnosis of the capitalistic economy:

1. There is nothing automatic in the actual developments of the economy which will pull it out of a depression — an economy in depression can remain so indefinitely.

2. Prosperity depends on savings being put to use — on investment — as otherwise, a descending spiral of contraction will result in depression.

3. *Investment cannot be counted on,* as it depends on the expansion of production by the businessman and he cannot be expected to increase production beyond demand for his products — *so the capitalistic economy continuously lives in the shadow of collapse.*

Keynes explained that in time of depression savings could not continue to accumulate — how could it continue to accumulate when there was less income to save from? Savings would actually dry up, reduced to a trickle rather than a flow. And just when funds were needed for Investment to stimulate the economy, there would be no Savings accumulation available. So the *"see-saw" theory* was invalid — *replaced by the "elevator" theory.* The "elevator" concept was that the economy could stand still at any level — just as an elevator may remain standing on the ground floor as well as reach the top floor of a building. What was worse, a Depression was a natural development, with every "boom" to be followed by depression. This was because to avoid depression the economy had to continue expanding — but capital expansion of any business was restricted by that business' market. So capital expansion did not move at an increasingly high level but rather in "spurts." Consequently, Keynes' book was as revolutionary as had been Adam Smith's and Karl Marx's. The classical view that Depression was only temporary was turned into the bleak view that Depression was inherent in the system itself, and that any Depression could be *permanent.*

Of course, a mind as vigorous as Keynes' would not stop there, with nothing but a dismal outlook for the future. A cure was provided. Keynes' thesis was that since a depression could be permanent, and the downward trend of the economy was bound to occur after a period of prosperity, *the cure was "priming the pump" through government action* — the deliberate undertaking of heavy government investment to stimulate the economy. By taking up the slack in capital goods spending whenever private enterprise was unable to expand, the government could insure the continuous movement of the economy on a high level of activity. Therefore, the government of a nation should incorporate this concept into its permanent plans — but this program of government spending should be used only when necessary, and then in such amounts as might be necessary.

Keynes had visited Washington in 1934 and had observed the New Deal methods of President Roosevelt to combat the Depression. This was a practical demonstration of his thesis, but since it was already in actual use, his book became a defense for such policies. The WPA (Works Progress Administration) and a host of other New Deal projects were designed specifically to "prime the pump." Such measures did increase the national income by 50% and made a large dent into the rolls of the unemployed. However, they failed in the long run to defeat the Depression. The number of unemployed still amounted to about nine million, and what finally ended the Great Depression was World War II. That the "pump-priming" measures had failed did not invalidate Keynes' thesis because such measures failed in the United States due to two factors. First, the government was not financially able to carry out government spending to the full extent necessary. Second — and completely unexpected — was the opposition of private enterprise, for business leaders were frightened by government intervention in the economy and they refused to cooperate by investing in capital expansion when the time came that they could do so.

Keynes next attacked one of the chief problems of World War II with his book, *How to Pay for the War.* Its thesis was quite simple, and original. It proposed a compulsory savings plan for wage-earners for the purchase of government bonds during the war — to be redeemed at the war's end. Thus, inflation would be defeated by putting into savings the extra war income, and prosperity at the end of the war would be stimulated by the flow of money available for the purchase of consumer goods from the cashing in of the bonds. In short, this cure was just the opposite to Keynes' cure for depression — for the situation in wartime was reversed. In the meantime, the costs of the war would be paid for by the government from the money received in the sale of the bonds. Nothing came of the plan, however, for the political leaders preferred to use the old methods of taxation and rationing, along with the purchase of bonds on a purely voluntary basis.

John Maynard Keynes, while termed "radical" by conservative economists, had nothing but scorn for socialism and communism. Opposed to

Marx's view that capitalism was doomed, Keynes believed in a policy of *"managed capitalism"* — a policy which he was convinced would invigorate and save capitalism. Basically, he was a conservative with one great aim — the creation of a capitalistic economy in which *its greatest threat, unemployment,* would be eliminated forever. Consequently, he can rightfully be called "the architect of Capitalism Viable" — the designer of a living capitalism capable of growing.

Commentary

The "sick world" of John Maynard Keynes was a world whose economy was "sick" as the result of the world-wide Depression which almost ruined world trade and brought many nations to the brink of bankruptcy. Exports fell, national banks failed, the leading countries of the world were forced to abandon the gold standard, foreign debts were repudiated, and mass unemployment developed. The result in Europe was a definite tendency toward dictatorial forms of government (in Germany, Austria, Rumania, etc.) and the less favored nations such as Germany, Italy, and Japan embarked upon a national policy of territorial expansion.

In the United States, with the background of the "Roaring Twenties" and the legacy of Coolidge prosperity, the air was one of pure optimism. Herbert Hoover — the President from 1929 to 1933 — promised "two chickens in every pot and two cars in every garage." Suddenly, the "Doomsday of Wall Street Prosperity" arrived without warning on October 24, 1929. By October 29th, sixteen million shares had been sold at the stock market with staggering losses; by November 13th, thirty billion dollars in capital values had vanished, and by the end of two months this figure had increased to forty billion dollars. Just prior to the "Wall Street Crash" the total value of stocks had been eighty-seven billion dollars — by March of 1933 it had dropped to only nineteen billion dollars. It was the "Great Crash" of the stock market which triggered the "Great Depression." The basic causes of the Depression were these:

1. Agricultural overexpansion — resulting in surpluses.

2. Industrial overexpansion — too many factories and too much machinery to meet normal demand.

3. Labor-saving machines — fewer and fewer workers produced more and more goods.

4. Capital surpluses — inequality in the distribution of the national income.

5. Overexpansion of credit — stock market speculation and installment buying.

6. Decline of international trade — made acute by high tariff policies.

7. Political unrest — contributing to the default of payments on foreign debts.

By 1930 in a typical industrial city in the United States, one out of every four factory workers had lost their jobs. In the major cities many working men and women slept at night in the public parks because their income was insufficient to provide for shelter. Residential construction had fallen off by 95%. By 1933 the depths had been reached, with over sixteen million workers unemployed out of a total population of only one hundred and twenty-odd million. Congressional leaders viewed events helplessly — stunned like the rest of the nation — and waited to see what the newly elected President might do.

This was the situation which witnessed the inauguration in March, 1933, of Franklin D. Roosevelt. He immediately called a special session which began the "Hundred Days" of emergency legislation under the President's slogan of "Relief, Recovery, and Reform." Such acts as the following became law: the Emergency Banking Act; the Federal Emergency Relief Administration; the Civilian Conservation Corps (CCC); the National Recovery Administration (NRA); the Agricultural Adjustment Act (AAA); the Federal Deposit Insurance Corporation (FDIC) — which guaranteed savings deposits in banks; the Federal Securities Act — which led to the SEC to regulate the stock market; the Home Owner's Loan Corporation (HOLC); and the Tennessee Valley Authority (TVA) — the prelude to a host of New Deal measures. Throughout, the New Deal philosophy was the concept of "priming the pump" through Federal Government action — which Keynes so ably defended in his major work, *The General Theory of Employment, Interest, and Money.* The result of the New Deal was that while the measures failed to end the Great Depression, the downward trend of the economy was halted and confidence was restored to the nation. Consequently, in a world featured by a solidified Communism and an aggressive Fascism, F. D. R. *saved* American capitalism. And this had been the goal all along of John Maynard Keynes' "managed Capitalism."

CHAPTER X

THE MODERN WORLD

Summary
    The economists whose views have been presented thus far were concerned primarily with what had taken place in the economic sphere in the past. They were able to point out the way in which the economic forces had operated because the outcome of those forces was already known. This was quite a different undertaking from that of making statements concerning

the future operation of these same forces. Keynes, however, in 1930 did venture a prediction concerning the course of the economy for future generations. In an essay entitled *Economic Possibilities for Our Grandchildren* he indicated that within the course of the next hundred years the economic problem might be solved. He believed that the capitalistic system would not only survive but its success would make available a relatively high standard of living for human beings the world over. This was in many respects a strange prediction for an economist to make especially at a time when the nations of the Western world were in the midst of a great depression. What was the basis or justification for it?

The answer to this question lies chiefly in his conviction that growth is the key to economic prosperity and in spite of the temporary fluctuations which have characterized economic history there has been growth in the process when viewed as a whole. This possibility of growth is bound to continue and if managed in the proper way it can bring about the state of affairs for which men of vision and courage have been hopeful. Keynes was well aware of the fact that the capitalistic system had not as yet been able to eliminate large areas of poverty or to prevent a Depression with its sagging prices and sluggish labor markets. Marxists had insisted that economic stagnation was an inevitable consequence of the capitalistic system, which would eventually destroy itself. They regarded the Depression of the thirties as evidence of the correctness of their analysis. Keynes did not accept their view. He pointed out that the Depression had been due in large measure to causes that could be corrected. One of these was the wild speculation which had brought about the crash of the stock market. Business and household loans had been based on the collateral of stocks priced far above their actual worth. When the crash came millions of middle-class people lost most of their savings and were left destitute. Another cause was what Keynes regarded as a mistaken economic policy on the part of the Federal Reserve Board. Fearing the danger of inflation, they advocated a tight-money policy which offered little encouragement for business enterprises to expand. This was the opposite of what they should have done. By making the supply of money available to those who were ready to expand the industries in which they were engaged, the growth of the economy would have been promoted. This conclusion was later verified by the revival of business which took place after the tight-money policy had been reversed and funds were available for expenditures on a large scale.

With the coming of the Second World War the inhibitions on the part of the government toward large-scale expenditures were removed and this, together with the accumulation of savings that had been acquired, made the money supply sufficient for the growth and expansion of all phases of the economy, thus enabling the Gross National Product to rise by a higher percentage than had ever been reached before. It is true that the economic prosperity of this period was largely due to the war and it was feared that the end of the war would bring not only a decrease in the demand for military expenditures but also an increase in the rate of unemployment that would have a serious effect upon the economy. These dangers were avoided to a large extent by new areas of expenditure on the part of the government. Money was provided for the building of roads, the establishment of hospitals, the development of educational opportunities for more people, the conservation of natural resources, and in general contributing to the welfare of the country as a whole. The growth of the economy as a result of these measures produced an attitude of optimism concerning the future of the capitalistic system. Under the continuing stimulus of both private and government spending, all of the capitalistic nations began to show evidence of steady growth. It appeared that the economic philosophy of Adam Smith had been rediscovered and revitalized. It had been shown that growth is the normal course for a market economy and the accumulation of capital is the driving force of the system.

There was, however, one important difference between the optimism of this period and the theory which had been advocated by the author of the *Wealth of Nations*. It had to do with the role of government in the economy. Smith had believed in the doctrine of *laissez faire,* which means that government should not interfere with the natural operation of economic forces. Its function so far as business is concerned should be limited to the active promotion of competition and the overcoming of any barriers to mercantilist privilege. This was not the view of Keynes nor any of the postwar economists. The problems which they envisioned were quite unknown to Adam Smith and they called for a different type of treatment. Instead of the government playing a passive role and allowing business to run its own course, they held that its proper function was to supply a supportive environment that would promote and encourage the growth of the capitalistic system.

Although growth in the economy was sufficient to pull capitalistic countries out of the Depression and may even serve as a preventive of a similar one occurring in the future, it is evident that it does not solve all of the economic problems. Growth is not a steady process in any economy and its ability to keep things moving forward varies a great deal from one country to another. Even though the Gross National Product is on the rise, this does not mean the abolition of ghettos or the complete elimination of unemployment. With all of its advantages, there is the ever-present danger of an inflation which cheapens if it does not ruin the purchasing power of the consumer. Thus the possibility exists that growth in the economy may be nothing more than the exchanging of one evil for another.

Any adequate survey of economic conditions in the postwar world will reveal the tendency to generate higher price levels for all kinds of consumer goods. This means a steady decline in the purchasing power of currencies. This situation has been brought about by institutional changes of far-reaching scope and effect. One of these is the presence of high rates of growth in all market systems. As a consequence of this high rate of growth, competing systems encounter shortages of both labor and materials, which cause prices to rise. Then, too, the fact that growth is sponsored and supported by government encourages the businessman to make expenditures involving risks that he would not think of taking by himself alone. He feels certain that regardless of the way his venture will turn out the government will see to it that another Depression is not in the making. Another factor which contributes toward the inflationary tendency is the altered occupational setting of modern economics. To a considerable extent the labor force of the present day is directed toward the production of services rather than the manufacture and distribution of material goods. People are employed as teachers, ministers, lawyers, hospital attendants, government workers, and in various other ways, none of which are directly involved in the increased production of consumable goods. In this respect they are quite different from the farmer, the coal miner, and the steel worker, who can always justify their demand for higher wages by the increased productivity of their work. The fact that those who perform services are unable to show any increased output of consumable goods does not lessen their demand for an income that is as high if not higher than that received by those engaged in a different line of work. As the price of goods continues to rise, there is bound to be an increased demand for higher wages. In many instances it can be shown that wages have been increased by a percentage that is considerably higher than the increased cost of living. Here, too, it can be pointed out that the cost of services has increased by an amount that exceeds the wages paid to the workers who are producing material goods. All of this adds greatly to the burden of inflation.

Without doubt the question of inflation is the dominant issue in the economics of the modern world. Will capitalism be able to solve this problem as well as it has succeeded in finding a solution for other ones? Not all economists are agreed that it can. A warning in this respect was set forth in 1932 when Adolph Berle and Gardner Means published the book entitled *The Modern Corporation and Private Property*. It was the thesis of this book that the rise of giant corporations and their control of a high percentage of the nation's wealth by a small group of directors and managers constituted a threat to the whole idea of competitive enterprise. They warned that "If a dominant tendency of American business continued for another fifty years, the traditional fabric of capitalism would be destroyed." Furthermore, they asserted that the rise of giant corporations pointed the way toward a kind of neo-feudalism in which the managers of these corporations would have the same absolute control of the economy as their medieval predecessors exercised over their smaller and weaker principalities. Without doing anything to check the dangers of inflation the trend toward larger and more powerful corporations carries the added threat of monopolistic control. Opponents of the Keynesian theory of economics had always insisted that large scale expenditures on the part of the government constituted a dangerous threat to the system of free enterprise. It was a policy that leads toward socialism and the loss of individual liberties.

More than thirty years have passed since Berle and Means issued their warning, and we are now able to assess the value of the predictions which they made. Although the growth of corporations has continued to some extent, the tendency toward monopolistic control has been held in check by a number of different factors. One of these has been the presence of antitrust laws which have caused corporations to shy away from attempts to corner the market of any particular commodity and thus become involved in an antitrust lawsuit. They have been able to do this partly through the emergence of conglomerates, which means that corporations have grown not by merging with other companies selling the same product but by combining with companies selling different products. Another important factor has been the continued existence of smaller-sized competitors within the fields dominated by a particular industry. While these factors do not mean that the consumer has complete protection from the dangers of inflation and monopoly, his freedom in the marketplace has not been restricted to the point that was anticipated. One of the reasons for this is the fact that growth in the number and size of corporations has been accompanied by a changed attitude in the nature of competition. It is not as ruthless as it was in the days of Karl Marx, when capitalists had to exploit labor in order to stay in business. Now it is characterized by a more humane policy of live and let live.

Another problem which is demanding a great deal of attention by economists in the modern world is that of the environment. This includes the relationship between the rate of growth in the world's population and the ability to obtain an adequate supply of food. The gloomy predictions of T. R. Malthus must be faced again but this time with some added factors to be taken into account. The world's supply of raw materials is limited, and even if it would be possible to bring the rate of population growth under control, it seems quite unlikely that the necessary mineral and power resources could be found to raise the standard of living in all of the so-called backward countries of the world to that which is recognized as adequate among the Western nations.

Commentary

When Keynes wrote his essay on the *Economic Possibilities for Our Grandchildren* the outlook for the future of capitalism was very dark. This was especially true in the United States. The stock market had crashed the year before; unemployment had reached a dangerous level; bank failures were numerous; and long bread lines were common in all of the large cities of the country. Marxian economists regarded this state of affairs as indicative of the inevitable collapse of the capitalistic system which their leaders had predicted more than a half century before. Keynes was convinced that this was not true. He was not blind to the failures of the system of free enterprise as it had been operating in the past, but he believed that these faults could be corrected without destroying the system itself. He recognized that the conditions which prevailed at the time of his writing constituted a real crisis, but capitalism had survived critical situations before and he was confident that it could do so again. As he saw it the Depression of the thirties had been brought about not so much by economic laws operating within the system of capitalism as it had by unwise decisions on the part of the people involved. The crash of the stock market had been caused by wild speculation and the overextension of various forms of credit. The sharp decline in the economy which followed the debacle in the stock market was due in part to unwise decisions by the managers of the Federal Reserve Board. Appropriate actions by the federal government could overcome these defects and prevent their happening again.

Keynes's hope for the future of capitalism was based on his firm belief that growth is the key to economic success. While the rate of growth has not been uniform throughout the period of economic history, its course for more than two centuries has been characterized by a steady upward climb. Keynes saw no reason why this trend could not be continued in a manner that would make the future of capitalism a period of expansion rather than one of stagnation, as had been predicted by the communists. This, in his judgment, would necessarily involve positive action by the federal government. It was not long until his theory was put into practice during the administration of President Franklin D. Roosevelt. Regulations concerning the economy were enacted by the federal government on a scale that far surpassed what had been done in previous administrations. Unemployment was reduced through the creation of new job opportunities sponsored by such agencies as the NRA, the AAA, the WPA, and others of a similar nature. Money was made available by the government for the protection of bank deposits and for the expansion of industries. All of this was a radical departure from the older policies of following the law of supply and demand and allowing economic factors to run their own course. Naturally political and economic conservatives were alarmed at the new turn of events, which they regarded as measures leading to socialism. Their protests may have had some influence in causing the Supreme Court to declare some of the new agencies that had been established unconstitutional. Nevertheless, the new applications of Keynesian economics were continued as the government kept on with large-scale expenditures of money for the promotion of growth in the economy.

That some growth in the economy did take place even in the decade of the twenties is evidenced by the fact that the Gross National Product rose from $104 to $110 billions. With the coming of the Second World War and the increased expenditures by the government for military purposes, it rose from $110 to $183 billions in terms of 1929 purchasing power. With the end of the war the need for military expenditures was greatly reduced and the return of soldiers from overseas added to the rate of unemployment. In view of these facts, it began to look as though the country was headed for another period of Depression. This, however, was averted as the government found new avenues for the expenditure of public funds. Roads, schools, and hospitals were financed in part by the federal government. Scores of projects designed to meet many of the more urgent needs of state and local communities were promoted in the same way. With the coming of the Korean War expenditures for military purposes were again increased. The Marshall Plan for the rehabilitation of war-torn European countries was another factor which required enormous sums of money for carrying out its purposes. Both public and private spending increased by leaps and bounds and through it all the Gross National Product in the United States continued to rise until it reached the almost unimaginable point of more than a trillion dollars a year. Similar effects, though on a smaller scale, have been experienced in European countries. In fact, it has been stated that as a result of this economic policy "all capitalist nations began to evidence steady growth; and under the influence of steady growth, all capitalist nations began to look to growth as a responsibility of their governments."

Although the Keynesian doctrine with reference to government spending was apparently successful in bringing the United States out of the Great Depression, it did not provide a solution for all of the economic problems that were bound to occur either in the immediate or the more distant future. It did not contain any safeguards against the dangers of an excessive inflation nor did it give any adequate protection from a form of socialism that would involve a serious curtailment of individual liberties. Both of these dangers have been recognized as constituting a threat to the survival of the capitalistic system in the modern world. Economists are faced with the problem of seeing how they can be met without sacrificing the essential elements of the system itself.

There can be no question about the problem of inflation being one of the major issues in the modern world. The rapid expansion of industries, along with the ever-increasing size of national debts, has been accompanied by a tendency of the world's economies to generate higher and higher price levels and thus to reduce the purchasing power of national currencies. As prices rise there is a corresponding demand for higher wages. The economies are involved in a vicious circle from which there appears to be no escape. The situation in the modern world is complicated by certain factors which have not been present in inflationary periods of the past. One of these is the presence of high rates of growth in all market systems. As a result of these steady rates of growth, economies are faced with the fact of sheer limitations in resources which are available. The supply of those commodities on which so much of our industries are dependent is by no means inexhaustible. Another important factor is the increased market power of both labor and industry. Corporations, while still competing with one another, do not resort to price warfare as they once did. Even in those instances when a strike is called, it is seldom if ever that a union has accepted a cut in wages as a result. Again, the changed occupational setting in modern economies has some bearing on the inflationary tendency, for a large percentage of the labor force has to do with services rather than the production of material goods. These laborers cannot claim, as other workers do, that their demand for higher wages is justified by increased production of goods, and yet statistics show that when the price level of commodities rose by 35% the price of service items rose by 50%. Whether the capitalistic system will be able to cope successfully with inflation is still an open question, even though the distribution by the federal government of Social Security benefits and their attempts to regulate wages and prices has eased the situation to some degree.

The rapidly increasing role of government in regulating the affairs of the market has caused many persons to fear that capitalism may be replaced by a socialistic economy. This fear is not without some foundation, but it is also possible that individual liberties may be curbed even more by monopolistic control on the part of huge corporations. A warning to this effect was set forth in the book *The Modern Corporation and Private Property* by Berle and Means. The authors of this book, alarmed by the tendency of corporations to merge into giant supercorporations thus eliminating to some extent the element of competition, warned that "If a dominant tendency of American business continued for another fifty years, the traditional fabric of capitalism would be destroyed." As they saw it "A society in which production is governed by blind economic forces is being replaced by one in which production is carried on under the ultimate control of a handful of individuals." This indicated to them a kind of economic feudalism in which the great mass of consumers are at the mercy of their economic overlords.

Although the power of these giant business enterprises in determining the conditions under which the vast majority of people will live is not something to be ignored, there are a number of factors which tend to hold them in check. One of them is the presence of antitrust laws. Another one is the continued existence of smaller-sized competitors within the different fields that are controlled by these so-called *oligopolies,* or business organizations that dominate the market for several different kinds of goods. Finally there is evidence of a relatively new and more humane attitude on the part of business organizations. Instead of the ruthless competition which Karl Marx had maintained was the only way capitalists could stay in business, we now find more of an attitude of live and let live. Corporations may even cooperate with labor unions in searching for better ways to improve working conditions. One of the reasons for this changed attitude as expressed by J. K. Galbraith is that "giant enterprise cannot live in a world of insecurity, high risk competition, and 'blind forces' inherent in the traditional conception of the market."

CHAPTER XI

BEYOND THE ECONOMIC REVOLUTION

Summary
This chapter is somewhat different from the preceding ones, for it has to do with factors that lie beyond the economic revolution. They are beyond in more than one sense of the word. They are beyond in point of time, for they are about situations occurring after the revolution has taken place. They are also beyond with reference to subject matter, for they are concerned with non-economic factors which nevertheless do have an important bearing on the future of the economic process. The chief topic under consideration is the question of whether or not the capitalistic system will be able to survive in the face of all the changing conditions that are taking place.

The discussion begins with an account of the views presented by Joseph Schumpeter, a distinguished economist who for several years was professor of economics at Harvard University. In a book called *Capitalism, Socialism, and Democracy,* which was published not long before his death, he stated his reasons for believing that capitalism will perish in the long run, even though he thought it might continue for another fifty or one hundred years. The message of the book was a surprise to many of his contemporaries, for Schumpeter had long been regarded as an admirer of the virtues of capitalism, with its emphasis on freedom and the rights of the individual. The decline of capitalism, in his judgment, was not due to the operation of economic factors alone but rather to these factors in combination with certain social and psychological elements in the environment. For capitalism to survive in the modern world its leaders must be imbued with the spirit of adventure. They must have the courage and the fortitude which was characteristic of the early pioneers. These qualities were no longer present among the "managers" who have replaced the former "captains of industry." These managers are the administrators of big business but their chief interest is in their own local welfare and they have little regard for the system as a whole or its relationship to the needs of the community. Big business has become conservative, not in its policies or social ideals, but in its economic daring. Capitalism has declined under a wave of skepticism which has swept the country. It has succumbed to the influence of intellectuals who have been saying that money is not the most important thing in life and "private property is no more sacred than the divine right of kings." From this point of view the business way of life has lost its attractiveness. Capitalism is in a state of decay brought about by the very civilization it has produced. When asked if he believes that capitalism can survive Schumpeter replies with candor "No, I do not think it can."

One of the most significant things about Schumpeter's position is the fact that he is the first economist to maintain that economic development alone does not determine the fate of capitalism. This is in many respects an entirely new point of view. Previously it had been held that the power of the purse was the driving force in the economy. Once the nature of economic forces and their manner of operation were clearly understood, it would be possible to foretell the future. Business cycles were not caused by human decisions. They were the result of fluctuations in the market, for economic history was to a large extent an automatic process in which the results of the struggle for wealth could be predicted with a fair degree of accuracy. It was on this basis that Adam Smith had predicted an era of abundance in the future of capitalism; Malthus and Ricardo had made their gloomy predictions; the Utopians had forecast the coming of an age of plenty; Marx had spoken of the coming struggle between labor and capital; Veblen had predicted a conflict between technician and financier; and Hobson had indicated the need for large sums of money for the development of overseas markets. The predictions had varied because different economists had emphasized different aspects of the process. Capitalism was understood to be operating in a society in which the needs for the future are left to an automatic system. The notion that motives other than economic should be allowed to intrude would have been regarded as the most rank form of heresy. This was what characterized the old order, but now that we are past the economic revolution, this way of looking at things has been changed.

Evidence of the changed attitude can be seen in the philosophy of John Stuart Mill. Although a staunch individualist and a champion of the system of free enterprise, he believed in the freedom of the individual to make his own decisions, and the choices made both separately and collectively were bound to have an important effect upon the course of the economy. Instead of the passive acceptance of whatever emerged in the economic process, it was what the people desired most of all that really mattered. What they desired might be better or it might be worse than what the unimpeded action of the market would produce but at any rate they were free to make choices. They could regulate competition and by so doing preserve the best elements of free enterprise, while eliminating its more objectionable features. By thus intervening in the normal course of the business cycle, they were able to prevent what Marx had regarded as the inevitable collapse of the capitalistic system. Freedom of choice on the part of individuals, along with government planning and the development of a sense of social responsibility on the part of business executives, are the main tools of the anti-economic moral impulse.

What changes will take place in the life-styles of people and in their attitudes toward private property no one can predict with certainty, but whatever they are we can be sure they will have some bearing on the future of the economy. Two issues of great importance are bound to be faced and upon their outcome our survival as a free economy will to a great extent be determined. The first one is the problem of political isolation. The fact is that by far the greater portion of mankind has had no direct contact with capitalism nor is it likely to have in the foreseeable future. Millions of people living in China, India, South America, and other parts of the world know little or nothing at all concerning the relationships that exist among people living in a capitalistic society under a system of free enterprise. They have heard about the living standards of the rich and in contrasting these with the hardships and poverty prevailing in their own countries they have developed an attitude toward capitalism that is harsh, crude, and exploitative. They have been led to believe that capitalistic countries are not only powerful but corrupt. They are arrogant and interested in other people only insofar as they can be used to serve their own selfish purposes.

Can this attitude on the part of the so-called backward and undeveloped countries be changed? Democracies have hoped and believed that this can be done. They have been bold to proclaim their interest in, and their love for, all mankind but their statements have not been convincing to the peoples to whom they have been addressed. Probably the chief reason for this is the fact that democratic societies, like all others, are judged not by what they say but by what they do. All too often their actions have not been in harmony with their idealistic professions, or at least that is the way it has often been interpreted by people living in foreign countries. Then, too, capitalism has had a formidable rival in communism. Communism appeals to poverty stricken countries because it offers quick relief from the hardships to which they have been subjected. It can do so by imposing strict control over all phases of the economic process. The fact that this can be done only at the expense of the personal liberties of the people does not seem to matter a great deal to those who have never experienced the freedoms made possible in a democratic country under a system of free enterprise. In contrast to the methods of communism, democracies do not offer a quick and easy solution to economic problems. The benefits which they promise are long-range benefits which are not purchased at the expense of individual liberties. From the point of view of the democracies the price of communistic benefits is entirely too high. They prefer the slower and often more painful method of a gradual change which involves voluntary choice rather than brute force.

For capitalism to be successful in its struggle against communism it must do something more than putting forth the claim that its political ideals are more noble and humanitarian than those of the communists. Both systems, according to their official spokesmen, have as their ultimate objective the alleviation of poverty and a higher standard of living for all of the peoples of the world. The real issue is which one of the two systems is in a better position to reach this objective? While communists are willing to employ revolutionary methods to achieve their goal, capitalists abhor the use of violence and rely instead on education and other non-violent forms of social improvement. They are confronted with the difficult task of persuading the dispossessed peoples of the world that they are as much concerned with their welfare as the communists and that in the long run their methods are more likely to succeed.

In addition to the problem of isolation, which is primarily a political one, there is another problem which is equally important for the future of capitalism. It is the problem of developing a sense of moral and social responsibility on the part of those who live in a democratic society. Prior to the economic revolution the matter of social responsibility was given relatively little attention. It was not considered to be the function of business to worry about its social obligations or the long-range consequences of the policies which they pursued. Responsibility was something that belonged to the government and it was essentially political rather than economic. Now the situation is quite different. Capitalism is no longer isolated from the rest of the world and if it is to provide hope and guidance for the countries it wishes to serve its social responsibilities must be recognized and met. The wealth which capitalistic countries have acquired carries with it a responsibility to make the proper use of it. It is becoming increasingly evident that the choices made by a free people constitute a determining factor for the future life of the world. Wealth is power and power can be used either for good or for evil purposes. The crucial question is whether democratic societies will use their opportunities in a manner that is favorable toward the moral and intellectual development of all peoples or squander them in an attempt to satisfy the demands of their own selfish and animal nature.

Concerning the role of economic philosophy in the future there is ample opportunity to learn from both the mistakes and the achievements of the past. No system of economics has been without its faults and yet each of them has served some useful purpose in relation to the conditions which prevailed at the time. Conditions are constantly changing and economic theory will need to be modified in the light of these changes. Although there are some who advocate extreme positions of either the *Right* or the *Left,* it appears quite unlikely they will win any large scale support. The errors involved in the *laissez-faire* doctrine of Adam Smith are too well known to be repeated and the same is true of the revolutionary teachings of Karl Marx. This does not mean that either of these opposed systems will be completely abandoned. Both are capable of a wide range of responses to contemporary conditions. Each of them appears to have gained something from the experiences of the other. It may be that a system will be evolved that combines the best features of each without including the worst faults of either. At any rate the best argument in support of any theory of economics is a clear demonstration of the fact that it has worked well in those places where it has been adopted.

Commentary
The publication of *Capitalism, Socialism and Democracy* by the Harvard economist Joseph Schumpeter was a significant event in the history of economic theory. Its distinguishing feature was the fact that it recognized more clearly than any of its predecessors the extent to which the economic life in any country is dependent on the will of the people involved. This was

one factor that, in the main, had been ignored by the earlier economists. They had assumed that economic factors alone were sufficient for predicting the future course of economic events. Furthermore, it had been taken for granted that man is essentially a selfish creature and in his search for his own happiness the pursuit of wealth constituted the driving motive for his actions. It was these assumptions that Schumpeter brought into question. If they were not well founded (and he did not think they were), the system that had been based on them would sooner or later be bound to collapse. It was for this reason he expressed his own opinion that capitalism would not survive for more than a century.

This analysis of the situation came as a surprise to many of his contemporaries, for Schumpeter had long been regarded as an admirer of the capitalistic system. His loss of faith in its future was not due to the operation of economic principles but rather to his observations concerning human nature and the way in which the economy of a country is influenced by the decisions of its people. Insofar as these decisions are made by free choices, there can be no definite predictions as to what they will be. Hence, the failure of capitalism to survive must not be regarded as something that is inevitable. The belief that it will eventually be replaced by some type of socialistic system was based on the changed attitudes he had observed concerning business practices and the reluctance of people in general to deny themselves the satisfactions of the moment for the sake of social welfare in the more distant future. The spirit of adventure which had been characteristic of the "captains of industry" was lacking among the more modern "managers" of business enterprises, who seemed to be more concerned about their own personal security than what might happen to the future of the system of free enterprise. He did not doubt that these attitudes could be changed, but he did question the willingness of people to make the changes necessary for the preservation of the system.

Before the economic revolution, the acquisition of wealth as an end in itself was seldom if ever brought into question. It was assumed that material prosperity was what all individuals as well as nations desired above everything else. Hence, it was the production of wealth and its proper distribution that for the most part occupied the attention of economists. Now a change was taking place. It was the use of wealth that was coming to be regarded as of equal importance with its accumulation and the way in which it was shared among the members of a given community. Then, too, it was being emphasized by intellectuals that money is not an end in itself. It is only a means toward some desired end. Insofar as the desired end is happiness, it was becoming evident that the mere possession of wealth is no guarantee of happiness. The wealthiest people in the world are not always the happiest ones and those who possess very little so far as material goods are concerned are often found to be happier than those who possess more. Happiness is obtained not so much by getting what one wants as it is by learning to control one's desires so that he will want only those things that are possible and in harmony with the best interests of himself as well as that of others. Important as these considerations are, they do tend to lessen the urge for acquiring wealth that was the driving motive of the capitalistic system. This was an added reason for Schumpeter's skepticism concerning its future.

It is impossible to foresee all of the new factors that will influence the future of capitalism but there are certain issues that will have to be faced. One of them is the problem of political isolation. It is especially important, for it is upon the solution provided for this problem that the future of the democratic process is dependent. It is an obvious fact that, with reference to the world's population, democratic countries are very much in the minority. There was a time when it seemed reasonable to believe that the non-democratic countries of the world would eventually change their system of government and become more nearly like the free nations of the Western world. In the words of President Woodrow Wilson at the time of the First World War, it was our objective to "make the world safe for democracy." Once this objective had been achieved and the masses of people were free to determine their own destiny, their standards of living would be raised until they approached the level enjoyed in the democratic countries. At the present time these hopes have almost disappeared. In view of the rapid rate of growth in the population of the undeveloped countries, it seems quite unlikely that the resources of nature are sufficient to provide a high standard of living for all the peoples of the world. This does not mean that it is impossible to improve the lot of those who are living in the so-called poorer countries, but any steps in the direction of their economic development will not take place without social and political change. Changes of this nature do not take place readily nor are they brought about through a smooth evolutionary process. On the contrary, they may involve violence and the acceptance of bold and ruthless dictatorships. They do not hold out much hope or encouragement for the development of democratically oriented and economically free societies.

While the loss of individual freedom cannot be accepted by the democratic countries of the West, it is not so objectionable to those countries that have never enjoyed a large degree of freedom. As a general rule they are suspicious of democracies, which they regard as hostile, arrogant, and attempting to impose their way of living on people who do not want it. They believe that democratic nations are interested in them not for the sake of promoting their welfare but rather for the purpose of exploiting their resources. They may abhor violence and the use of revolutionary methods, but it often happens that they see no other way of overcoming the miseries to which they have been subjected. It remains the task of democratic countries to change their attitudes by convincing them that the freedom-loving nations are really interested in their welfare and are willing to promote it even at the expense of their own economic interests. Obviously, it will take more than words to do this, for people are judged not so much by what they say as by what they do. It may be, as Heilbroner has suggested, that they will first of all need to convince themselves that this is true.

A second issue that will have to be met by democracies is the problem concerning their social responsibilities. Recognizing that their future as well as that of other countries is becoming to an increasing extent the object of their own selection, the areas of their social and moral responsibilities take on new and enlarged dimensions. The wealth acquired through technological developments and economic mechanisms makes them morally accountable for the way in which it is being used. The coexistence even within their own borders of poverty and abundance, of luxury and lack of essentials for a decent standard of living, are conditions for which they cannot claim to be entirely innocent. It is in this connection that Heilbroner says "If anything is in scarce supply in the United States today, it is not the means, but the will, to remedy the malfunctions of the economic process." It is not merely a question of which system, capitalism or socialism, will outlast the other, but rather which one can make the adaptations that will the more adequately serve the needs of the people. Both systems are capable of making a wide range of responses. These may be humane or inhumane and progressive or reactionary. Their success or failure will be determined in no small degree by the traditions and political genius of the respective countries in which they are operating.

FINAL SUMMARY AND EVALUATION OF WORK

The Worldly Philosophers is a tremendous book, a book which should be required reading not only of college students, but of every person who wishes an understanding of the economic system under which he lives. Basically, the book offers three things.

First, it offers a simple but comprehensive explanation of the ideas of the Great Economists. In doing so, it gives the reader an insight into the lives of these men, as well as a valuable summary of the history of their time. Thus, their concepts are placed into the proper context which explains how their philosophies were guided and motivated by their personal experiences with the historical events which swept their era. Throughout his work, Robert L. Heilbroner has woven into the narration the freshness of approach, the wit, and the originality which make for interest on the part of the reader. Economic concepts are portrayed in a non-technical way and their treatment is one which fascinates. Consequently, the reading of the book is not only an interesting, but an enjoyable experience.

Secondly, the book offers a valuable introduction to the student who will be studying any course in economics. Such students will find that the basic explanation of capitalism, of socialism, of communism, of prosperity and depression, and of the practical workings of economic activities is all contained in this text. And in marked contrast to the dry, technical, and almost purely theoretical treatment of the subject of economics by the usual textbook, *The Worldly Philosophers* gives a vibrant and most practical explanation of how the world of economics was, how it is today, and how it might be in the future. Any student who studies this book in a course on the social sciences in general, will find it extremely profitable to re-study the book prior to taking a course in economic principles and problems.

Finally, for the person who wishes to be "educated" — to understand something of the world in which he lives, and how this world has come about — this book is "must" reading. It is much more than a history of the lives, times and ideas of the great economic thinkers of the Western World, and much more than a highly readable explanation of basic economic principles. It presents political, social, and ethical concepts along with its description of economic thought, and all are ingeniously blended into a real contribution to modern man's understanding of his society.

DEFINITIONS OF SIGNIFICANT TERMS AND CONCEPTS

The following definitions and explanations of significant terms and concepts are not arranged in alphabetical order, but in the order in which they appear in each chapter.

CHAPTER II

Economics
The study of the ways in which man makes a living; the study of human wants and their satisfaction; the science of wealth.

Economic System
The rules, laws, customs, and principles which govern the operation of an economy. Each economic system has its own peculiar problems and therefore produces its own solutions.

Economic Activity
All action concerned with the creation of goods and services to be in some way consumed.

Consumption
The process by which goods and services are utilized in satisfying man's needs and wants.

Production
The process of creating the goods or services to be consumed.

Distribution

a. "Physical"
The process of getting these goods and services into the hands of those who need them or want them for consumption.

b. "Personal"
The division of *income* among persons, classified by size.

c. "Functional"
The division of *income* according to different types — wages, rent, interest, profit.

Basic Agents (Factors) of Production:
Land, Labor, Capital (and Management).

Land
Natural resources.

Labor
Human effort.

Capital
The physical necessities for production — buildings, machinery, tools, equipment, supplies; the layman generally views this as the necessary money for these purposes.

Management
The planning, coordinating, and direction of production.

The Economic Revolution
The development of historical factors which culminated in the adoption of the market system (capitalism).

Factors Responsible for the Economic Revolution:

The Renaissance
(1350-1600) — particularly through the decay of the restrictive religious spirit in favor of a skeptical, inquiring attitude.

The Scientific Revolution
(1500-1700) — laying the foundations for the Industrial Revolution.

The Emergence of Nation-States
(15th, 16th, and 17th centuries) — giving rise to royal patronage for favored industries, maritime trade, and to common laws, common measurement, and common currencies.

The Age of Exploration and Discovery
(15th, 16th, and 17th centuries) — providing natural wealth in gold and silver, and raw resources from the colonies.

The Protestant Reformation
(1500-1648) — by encouraging enterprise, the investment of capital, and making "interest" and "profit" respectable.

CHAPTER III

Age of Enlightenment
A period (roughly 1700-1789) when political, economic, and social thought was dominated by an optimistic faith in reason and in the progress of the human race.

Mercantilism
The doctrine which dominated European economic policies from 1500 until the advent of "laissez faire" through a program which stressed that the real wealth of a nation resulted from its stores of gold and silver, which could be acquired by an excess of exports to imports, self-sufficiency of the nation, and exploitation of colonies.

Physiocrats
A group of thinkers of the Age of Enlightenment who were opposed to Mercantilism, believing instead that the true source of wealth was from land and agriculture, and who advocated the doctrine of "laissez faire."

François Quesnay
French philosopher of economics who founded the school of Physiocrats and greatly influenced Adam Smith.

Laissez Faire
Literally means "to be left alone" — the economic doctrine founded by Quesnay and the Physiocrats and expounded by Adam Smith, stressing no interference in the operations of the market economy.

Three Historical Stages of Capitalism:

First Stage
(1450-1650): *"Commercial Capitalism"* — profits made from the transportation of goods.

Second Stage
(1750-1870's): *"Industrial Capitalism"* — profits made from the manufacturing process itself; *coincides with the "Industrial Revolution."*

Third Stage
(1880's to present): *"Financial Capitalism"* — profits made from the investment of finance capital.

Industrial Revolution
Term used to describe the transition from the stable agricultural and commercial society of the Western world to the modern industrialized society — the second stage of capitalism.

Enclosure Movement
The practice of fencing off lands formerly subject to common rights in order to provide pasture land for sheep — causing a shift of the poor in England to cities.

Patron Saint of Free Interprise
Adam Smith.

Father of Modern Economics
Adam Smith.

Classical Economists
The economists who preached the doctrine of "laissez faire" and stressed that the production, consumption, and distribution of goods and wealth were determined exclusively by economics "laws" and principles, to the exclusion of any social considerations.

CHAPTER IV

Iron Law of Wages
Labor's wages must remain at the subsistence level — its "natural price" — because of the workingman's tendency to increase his offspring. (David Ricardo)

Malthusian Doctrine
Thomas Malthus' thesis that population, unless checked, grows at a greater rate than the means of subsistence. Final result — starvation.

Neo-Malthusianism
Name originally used for "birth control."

CHAPTER V

Founder of British Socialism
Robert Owen.

Founder of French Socialism
Saint-Simon.

Utopia
Name comes from Sir Thomas More's fictional work, *Utopia,* and is used to describe any social, intellectual, or political scheme which is impractical at the time when it is conceived and presented; also used to refer to those *ideal states* which are impossible to realize because they are peopled by ideal human beings, and because they are based generally on what the author thinks *ought to be,* rather than on what actually is.

Socialism
Means the state ownership of the basic means of production, and the nationalization of all land, forests, and minerals, public transportation, trade, and banking, as well as the means of production—with the profits which formerly went to capitalists and landlords to now go to the people as a whole, through the State. This goal *is to be attained through peaceful evolution, without the loss of personal liberty.*

Utopian Socialists
Reformers who were inspired largely by the ideas of the "Enlightenment" and the French Revolution, particularly the belief in progress and in the perfectibility of man. They wished to reform their society by voluntary means—which earned for them the scorn of Karl Marx who dismissed them as visionary idealists, giving them the name, "utopian socialists."

Democratic Liberalism
A broad-minded view of the principles of "laissez faire" which modified its principles; chief spokesman was John Stuart Mill.

CHAPTER VI

Hegelian Dialectics
The philosophical concept that *in the world of ideas* change occurred as the result of a synthesis of opposing forces: a given idea *(Thesis),* when challenged by a new and opposing idea *(Antithesis),* would result in a new concept *(Synthesis)* which was somewhat closer to the truth than the initial two ideas.

Dialectical Materialism
Known as the "Marxian dialect" and "inverted Hegelism," this was Karl Marx's substitution of realism for Hegel's idealism—applying the dialectical method to an explanation of all world events.

Historical Materialism
Marx's *"economic interpretation of history"* which stressed economics as the basis for all human actions and historical events.

Communism
The belief in the achievement of the goals of socialism by *revolutionary means,* with the preaching of *class warfare.*

Marxism
The gospel of Communism according to the exact words and predictions of Karl Marx.

Scientific Socialism
What Marx and Engels called their ideas, as expressed in *The Communist Manifesto* and *Das Kapital,* termed "scientific laws" which explained the economic determination of history, the class struggle, and the inevitable downfall of capitalism with the triumph of the proletariat class.

Prophet of the Proletariat
Karl Marx.

Capitalists
The class which provides or controls the capital for the production of goods. While technically the upper class of the "bourgeoisie"—known as the "haute bourgeoisie"—to Marxists this class has become the "upper" class to be hated.

Bourgeoisie
This term generally used to mean *the middle class,* but technically it includes the "petite bourgeoisie"—the small shopkeepers, government officials, lawyers, doctors, independent farmers, and teachers—and the "haute bourgeoisie." Generally used by the Marxists to describe people with private property. ("Bourgeois" is the spelling when used as an adjective.)

Proletariat
The class of lowly wage earners—the workers.

Anarchism
The belief that all forms of government, controls, or authority are oppressive—so the ideal is *no* government.

Father of Anarchism
Pierre Proudhon.

CHAPTER VII

The Victorian Age
The period associated with the reign of Queen Victoria of Great Britain, 1837-1901.

Imperialism

The extension of authority or control — whether direct or indirect — of one people over another.

Economic Imperialism

The economic and/or political domination of underdeveloped countries by powerful nations, with the motive being economic; took place between 1870 and 1914 — known as *"Europe's Golden Age of Imperialism."*

CHAPTER VIII

Robber Barons

Term to describe the unscrupulous titans of finance and industry in the U.S., such as Jay Gould, Jim Fisk, and Cornelius Vanderbilt, when capitalism began to flourish in the United States; taken from title of the book by Matthew Josephson.

Technocracy

The belief in government being run by technical experts, with money replaced by "work units" of currency.

CHAPTER IX

The Great Crash

The *"Wall Street Crash"*: October, 1929, when the New York Stock Exchange was hit by a selling wave in which the values of stocks, which had reached an all-time high, came tumbling down in panic.

The Great Depression

Triggered by the "Wall Street Crash," there was a world-wide depression from 1930 to 1939, the depths of which were reached in 1933 in the United States.

The New Deal

The social and economic reforms carried out by President Franklin D. Roosevelt between 1933 and 1939 to combat the Great Depression.

The Hundred Days

The period of remarkable cooperation between F.D.R. and Congress — beginning with the special session of March 9, 1933 — when the basic measures of the "Relief, Recovery, and Reform" program of the New Deal were enacted into law.

CHAPTER X

Monopoly
Literally means "single seller"; one firm controls entire market.

Oligopoly
Literally means "a few sellers"; entire market controlled by just a very few firms.

CHAPTER XI

Gross National Product (GNP)
The best measure of the productivity of a country—in the United States it means the money value of all the goods and services produced in a given year.

SELECTED EXAMINATION QUESTIONS

1. The common interest of the "worldly philosophers" was their:

   a. worldly success and universal fame.
   b. philosophic use of logic in presenting their theses.
   c. concern with the historical development of economic man.
   d. concern over the value of labor.
   -e. concern over man's drive for wealth.

2. Which one is described as "a tramp"?

   a. Adam Smith
   b. David Ricardo
   c. Saint-Simon
   -d. Henry George
   e. Thorstein Veblen

3. Which one was known as "the man who educated Commons"?
   a. Adam Smith
   -b. David Ricardo
   c. Saint-Simon
   d. Henry George
   e. Thorstein Veblen

4. The "market system" refers to:

a. the many markets and fairs held in medieval Europe.
b. the economic system which was the foundation for feudalism.
-c. a society held together by the free action of profit-seeking individuals.
d. the extensive bartering of primitive tribes.
e. the New York Stock Exchange.

5. "Laissez faire" is to Adam Smith as "Managed capitalism" is to:

a. Thomas Malthus
b. David Ricardo
c. Henry George
-d. John Maynard Keynes
e. Joseph Schumpeter

6. Author of the pessimistic view that mankind would not be able to feed its growing population unless "moral restraint" was applied was:

-a. Thomas Malthus
b. David Ricardo
c. Henry George
d. John Maynard Keynes
e. Joseph Schumpeter

7. Author of the "Single Tax" as a panacea for the ills of society was:

a. Thomas Malthus
b. David Ricardo
-c. Henry George
d. Robert Owen
e. Thorstein Veblen

8. In the *Wealth of Nations;* the following were stressed as being bene-ficial to society:

a. Laws of the Market
b. Law of Accumulation and Law of Population
c. Division and specialization of Labor
-d. all of the above
e. (a) and (b), but not (c)

9. Who was known for his theory of "Dialectical Materialism"?
a. G. W. F. Hegel
-b. Karl Marx
c. Pierre Proudhon
d. Charles Fourier
e. John Maynard Keynes

10. Author of the idea that there was no automatic safety switch built into the economy to prevent a permanent depression was:

   a. Thorstein Veblen
   b. John Stuart Mill
-c. John Maynard Keynes
   d. Joseph Schumpeter
   e. Charles Fourier

11. Author of the "discovery" that the distribution of wealth could be arranged by each society, independently of economic "laws" was:

   a. Thorstein Veblen
-b. John Stuart Mill
   c. John Maynard Keynes
   d. Joseph Schumpeter
   e. Charles Fourier

12. Who described in great detail what is meant by the phrase "conspicuous consumption"?

-a. Thorstein Veblen
   b. John Stuart Mill
   c. John Maynard Keynes
   d. Joseph Schumpeter
   e. Pierre Proudhon

13. Which one is best remembered for his thesis of "priming the pump"?

   a. Thorstein Veblen
   b. John Stuart Mill
-c. John Maynard Keynes
   d. Joseph Schumpeter
   e. Pierre Proudhon

14. The expression, "a ship without a captain" best describes:

-a. capitalism
   b. socialism
   c. communism
   d. ancient Egyptian society
   e. most modern Latin American countries

15. Thorstein Veblen's hope for the future salvation of the economy was:

   a. the "Robber barons"
-b. the engineers

c. the capitalist
d. the consumer
e. the labor leader

16. An avid New Dealer would be apt to approve of the thesis of:

a. *Mathematical Psychics*
b. *The Road to Serfdom*
c. *A Treatise on Money*
-d. *The General Theory of Employment, Interest, and Money*
e. none of the above.

17. Who said, "Property is Theft"?

a. G. W. F. Hegel
b. Karl Marx
-c. Pierre Proudhon
d. Friedrich Engels
e. Saint-Simon

18. According to the German economist, Joseph Schumpeter, capitalism will:

a. be replaced by "Technocracy"
b. be able to meet all challenges successfully
c. win over the majority of the world, except for Russia and China
-d. be replaced by socialism
e. return to the adventurous spirit of the "captains of industry"

19. According to David Ricardo, the "villain" in the economic struggles in the market system was the:

a. worker
b. government
c. capitalist
d. banker
-e. landlord

20. Veblen believed that the businessman was being displaced by the:

a. government
b. worker
-c. machine
d. highly organized labor unions
e. onward march of socialism

A GUIDE TO FURTHER READING

For a thorough understanding of the history of economic theory there is no substitute for a careful reading of the major works written by the great economists. For the average reader who is not an economist but who wishes to pursue the subject a bit further than what is provided in these Notes the following list is recommended.

GALBRAITH, J. K. *The Affluent Society*. New York: The Houghton Mifflin Co., 1958. A widely used account of capitalism in the United States.

GEORGE, HENRY. *Progress and Poverty*. New York: Doubleday & Co. Inc., 1926. The most important and influential book written by the advocate of the single-tax idea.

HEILBRONER, ROBERT L. Englewood Cliffs, New Jersey: Prentice-Hall Inc., 1972. A simplified account of the history of economics. Appropriate for beginners.

_____. *Between Socialism and Capitalism*. New York: Vintage Books, Random House, 1970. A recent attempt to look into the future of capitalism.

KEYNES, JOHN MAYNARD. *Essays in Persuasion*. New York: Harcourt Brace & Co., 1951. A good introduction to the Keynesian theory of economics.

LEKACHMAN, ROBERT. *The Age of Keynes*. New York: Random House, 1966. An informative account of the economic situation in the Western world which forms the background for understanding the Keynesian theory.

MALTHUS, THOMAS R. *On Population*. New York: Modern Library, Random House, 1960. The Malthusian theory concerning population as set forth by its author.

MILL, JOHN STUART. *Autobiography*. New York: Columbia University Press, 1944. A real classic which presents the background for his famous essays *On Liberty* and *Utilitarianism*.

SAMUELSON, PAUL A. *Economics: An Introductory Analysis*. New York: McGraw-Hill, 1971. Strongly recommended as one of the best introductions to the study of economics.

SHERMAN, HOWARD. *Radical Political Economy*. New York: Basic Books, 1972. A good introduction to the study of the Marxian economic theory.

VEBLEN, THORSTEIN. *Theory of the Leisure Class*. New York: Modern Library, 1934. The best known work of this author.

NOTES

NOTES